# Survey of Corporate Contributions, 1988 Edition

## (An Analysis of Data for the Calendar Year 1986)

*by Linda Cardillo Platzer*

This report is based on data from the Annual Survey of Corporate Contributions, which is cosponsored by The Conference Board and the Council for Aid to Education.

*A Research Report from The Conference Board*

# Contents

## Charts

## Appendix Tables

## Acknowledgments

Many individuals have contributed their efforts to the success of this project—members of the Survey Research, Editorial Services, Charting, Production, and Office Services Departments. Special thanks go to Laura Adams, Andy Ashwell, Henrie Benin, Joe Convery, Steve Gazis, Lucy Langer, Joann Lemon, Selma Mackler, Eleanor Rizzo, Evelyn Samore, and Kim Wood.

# From the President

Charitable contributions activities by the nation's leading corporations have reached a watershed. An extraordinary growth rate that often reached double-digits in the 1970s and early 1980s has eroded steadily since 1985. The response from major corporations to this *Survey of Corporate Contributions* points to almost *no real growth* in 1986 and 1987. This trend calls for creative approaches to stretch the benefits of every contributions dollar.

The Conference Board's *Survey of Corporate Contributions,* now in its twenty-first edition, provides executives with a detailed, comprehensive overview of contributions practices based on information provided by 372 firms. As a budgeting and planning tool, this report enables executives to assess their own programs against those of other firms in their own industry, with the same income or asset size, or in their region of the country.

The report takes a particularly close look at industry differences—actual and anticipated changes in contributions activity, cash and noncash forms of giving, corporate as-sistance activity, foundation formation, and priorities among the major beneficiaries of corporate support. Also included is detailed information on subcategories of beneficiaries, with special tables on corporate funding of federated campaigns, particularly the United Way.

This report also introduces many new charts that present important highlights graphically and succinctly. Trends in noncash contributions, corporate assistance, foundation grants, and corporate priorities, for example, are now easier to follow through newly designed charts. Relationships between contributions levels and pretax income also emerge more clearly on charts developed for this edition.

The Conference Board is grateful to the contributions executives who participate every year in this survey. Their sustained support is essential to the quality of information we are able to report.

JAMES T. MILLS
*President*

# Highlights

For the second year in a row, charitable contributions by the nation's leading corporations grew only slightly, and expectations for the future continue to be limited. Real growth in corporate contributions in 1986 was almost nonexistent, as companies maintained their charitable giving programs but failed to sustain the extraordinary growth rate of the decade between 1976 and 1985.

Respondents to this *Survey of Corporate Contributions* indicated that 1986 was a year of stability, both in the size of contributions budgets and in the mix of cash and non-cash donations made by their companies. The major changes that occurred were in the reordering of priorities, as companies shifted funds among beneficiaries. The size of the contributions pie increased only slightly, but the shares apportioned to each of five major groups of nonprofit organizations underwent some substantial adjustments.

The major findings of the 1986 survey were:

• Contributions by all U.S. corporations for 1986 are estimated to reach $4.5 billion, an increase over 1985 contributions of less than 1% in constant dollars and the smallest increase since 1975.

• Companies in the matched sample of the survey reported a modest gain of just over 1% in real terms, continuing a slowdown that began in 1985. Corporate worldwide pre-tax income for the matched-sample companies overall fell by nearly 14% in 1986, following a 3% drop in 1985. The brakes that have been placed on contributions growth in recent years certainly reflect the economic performance of reporting companies.

• Respondents to the survey estimated that their final 1987 budgets would register an overall drop of 3%, with 40% of participants indicating that they expected cutbacks. However, estimates in the past have tended to be conservative, and it is likely that total corporate charitable giving in 1987 will be about the same as 1986.

• The share of giving to education surged from 38% to 43% of total contributions, the highest level in the history of the survey. Corporate contributions to education continue to be predominantly donations to *higher* education, which has traditionally received the lion's share of educational gifts. In 1986, higher education alone—including institutional operating grants, departmental and research grants, capital gifts, student financial aid, and matching gifts—captured nearly one-third of all corporate contributions reported in the survey.

Corporate awareness and interest in elementary and secondary education has been heightened recently. This was demonstrated by the leadership roles being taken by some corporations and by a Committee for Economic Development report that urges corporate involvement in preparing the next generation at an early age with the skills needed to prosper in tomorrow's economy. That message has not yet translated into measurable changes in the amount of support that corporations are putting into the nation's schools, however. Precollege educational institutions received slightly more than 2% of total contributions in 1986, up marginally from 1984 contributions. It may be several more years before the corporate commitment to early education now being articulated is reflected in corporate contributions.

• Corporate giving to health and human services organizations, including federated campaigns, such as United Way, continued to slip in share of total contributions. With the exception of 1985, corporate grantmaking in this category has been in steady decline for over a decade, falling from a high of 42% of total contributions in 1972 to only 28% in 1986.

• Civic and community organizations also lost share, declining from nearly 17% in 1985 to 13% in 1986. In the early 1980s, groups in this category were the recipients of several large real estate gifts—tracts of land or empty manufacturing and office facilities. There were fewer and smaller of such property gifts in 1986 and, thus, a reduction in both the amount and the proportion of total giving that went to civic and community activities.

# Methodology

## Sample

The Conference Board asked 1,200 top U.S. firms to participate in its 1986 *Annual Survey of Corporate Contributions*. Questionnaires were sent to the companies that appeared on the 1987 *Fortune* 500 list of the country's largest manufacturers and to those on the *Fortune* 500 list of service firms. An additional 200 companies, which were identified from published lists of the leading companies in each major industry sector, were also polled. Seventy-three percent of the respondents to the 1986 survey had also participated in the survey for 1985.

A total of 372 companies returned the questionnaire for 1986, representing a response rate of 31 percent. The aggregate contributions reported by these companies amount to 37 percent of the total contributions made by over half a million corporations reporting such gifts to the Internal Revenue Service. (See Appendix Table 1 on page 35.)

## Respondent Profile

The companies that regularly participate in The Conference Board's survey are among the country's major corporate contributors and their practices represent those of *leading* U.S. corporations. More than half of the 1986 survey participants made contributions in excess of $1 million each (Table A-1).

Approximately half of the respondents are manufacturing companies. Of those, nearly 84% are on the 1987 *Fortune* 500 list and over 70% have worldwide sales of over $1 billion.

Over 90% of the nonmanufacturing respondents in banking, insurance, telecommunications, and utilities reported assets of over $1 billion. Among those service companies whose size is measured by sales volume, 71% have sales over $1 billion. The 105 participants that appeared on the *Fortune* Service 500 list represent 58% of the service companies in the survey.

Other characteristics of the respondent population are described in Tables A-2 through A-5.

## Survey Administration

Every other year since 1978, The Conference Board has used an expanded questionnaire in order to obtain detailed information on subcategories of beneficiaries of corporate support. The Board used this expanded questionnaire for the 1986 *Annual Survey*. The questionnaire was mailed in March 1987, and addressed to a named contributions executive when a name was available. If no name was available, the covering letter was sent to the "Corporate Contributions Executive." Nonrespondents were sent a reminder letter in April, followed by one or more telephone calls in May and June. The cutoff date for participation was August 1, 1987. The questionnaire requested information concerning company size and financial performance, foundation assets, company direct giving and company foundation programs, cash and noncash giving, overseas giving, giving to detailed subcategories of the the five major categories of beneficiaries (for definitions, see page 20), and details on corporate assistance expenditures.

In years when the expanded form of the questionnaire for the *Annual Survey* is administered, as for this report, there are usually a number of companies that are unable to complete the detailed subcategories of giving. A total of 40 companies reported only category totals; other companies, although able to supply some of the subcategory data, could not identify some portion of their giving within the major categories. In each of these cases, the missing information was labeled "subcategory unidentified" to distinguish it from the subcategory "other."

## Table A-1: Profile of Participating Companies by Size of Contributions Program, 1984 to 1986

| Program Size | 1986 | | 1985 | | 1984 | |
|---|---|---|---|---|---|---|
| | Number | Percent | Number | Percent | Number | Percent |
| Less than $500,000 . . . . . . . . . | 87 | 23% | 116 | 27% | 146 | 34% |
| $500,000 to $1 million . . . . . . . | 72 | 19 | 79 | 18 | 75 | 18 |
| $1 million to $5 million . . . . . . . | 128 | 35 | 164 | 37 | 134 | 32 |
| $5 million and over . . . . . . . . . . | 85 | 23 | 80 | 18 | 67 | 16 |
| Total . . . . . . . . . . . . . . . . . . . | 372 | 100% | 439 | 100% | 422 | 100% |

**Table A-2: Survey Participants—**
Grouped by Worldwide Sales, 1986

| Worldwide Sales | Manufacturing Companies | | Selected Nonmanufacturing Companies[1] | |
|---|---|---|---|---|
| | Number | Percent | Number | Percent |
| Below $250 million | 4 | 2% | — | — |
| $250-500 million | 13 | 7 | 1 | 4% |
| $500 million-1 billion | 31 | 17 | 8 | 31 |
| $1 billion-2.5 billion | 50 | 27 | 4 | 15 |
| $2.5 billion-5 billion | 34 | 18 | 7 | 27 |
| $5 billion and over | 53 | 29 | 6 | 23 |
| Total | 185 | 100% | 26 | 100% |

[1]Excludes banks, insurance companies, telecommunications and utilities companies, which are grouped by Assets in Table A-3.

**Table A-3: Survey Participants in Banking, Insurance, Telephone, Gas and Electric Utilities,**
Grouped by Worldwide Assets, 1986

| Worldwide Assets | Banking | | Insurance | | Telephone, Gas and Electric Utilities | |
|---|---|---|---|---|---|---|
| | Number | Percent | Number | Percent | Number | Percent |
| Under $250 million | — | — | — | — | — | — |
| $250-$500 million | — | — | 2 | 5% | — | — |
| $500 million-1 billion | — | — | 5 | 12 | 6 | 10% |
| $1 billion-2.5 billion | 7 | 15% | 4 | 10 | 14 | 24 |
| $2.5 billion-5 billion | 7 | 15 | 7 | 17 | 13 | 22 |
| $5 billion-10 billion | 11 | 23 | 9 | 21 | 14 | 24 |
| $10 billion and over | 22 | 47 | 15 | 36 | 11 | 19 |
| Total | 47 | 100% | 42 | 100% | 58 | 100% |

**Table A-4: Comparison of Manufacturing Companies in 1986 Survey with Those in the *Fortune* 500 List — Companies Grouped by *Fortune* Ranking (Based on Total Worldwide Sales)**

| Company Rank | Number of Survey Respondents |
|---|---|
| Number 1- 100 | 68 |
| 101- 200 | 39 |
| 201- 300 | 26 |
| 301- 400 | 16 |
| 401- 500 | 12 |
| Total | 161 |

**Table A-5: Comparison of Nonmanufacturing Companies in the 1986 Survey with Those on the *Fortune* Service 500 List—Companies Grouped by Industry Class**

| Industry Class (Top 500) | Number of Survey Respondents |
|---|---|
| Top 100 diversified service companies (ranked by sales) | 10 |
| Top 100 commercial banking companies (ranked by assets) | 31 |
| Top 50 savings institutions (ranked by assets) | 0 |
| Top 50 life insurance companies (ranked by assets) | 19 |
| Top 50 diversified financial companies (ranked by assets) | 9 |
| Top 50 retailing companies (ranked by sales) | 7 |
| Top 50 transportation companies (ranked by operating revenues) | 5 |
| Top 50 utilities (ranked by assets) | 24 |
| Total | 105 |

## Chapter 1
# Moderation and Stability in Corporate Contributions Budgets

Corporate charitable contributions in 1986 advanced modestly over 1985 levels—in real terms, less than 1% for all U.S. corporations (Chart 1) and just over 1% for the leading companies surveyed by The Conference Board. The slowdown was not as severe as contributions executives anticipated, but does continue a pattern of retrenchment that began in 1985.

The current picture contrasts strongly with the extraordinary rise in corporate giving from 1976 to 1985—when contributions increased by 56% (in real terms) at the same time that corporate income before taxes *declined* 27% (Chart 1).

Chart 1:

## Corporate Contributions and Corporate Income Before Taxes in Current and Constant Dollars, 1972 to 1986

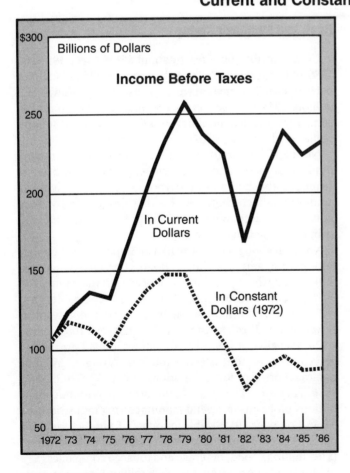

Source: U.S. Department of Commerce

Source: Internal Revenue Service; 1985 and 1986 estimate by Council for Aid to Education.

According to the Council for Aid to Education, total charitable contributions by all U.S. corporations are estimated at $4.5 billion for 1986 (see Appendix Table 1, page 35). This less than 1% rise in constant dollars over 1985 represents the lowest growth since 1975.

Chart 2 tracks the percentage change, adjusted for inflation, of both corporate contributions and corporate income before taxes between 1972 and 1986. While contributions levels have avoided the deep troughs in the income trend line, they nevertheless followed the general trend of changes in corporate income before taxes. Until 1980 (and especially between 1976 and 1979), contributions rose or fell at about the same rate as income before taxes. Contributions fell less sharply than income in 1980 and 1981 and then posted a gain of 9% in 1982, when corporate income before taxes plummeted 29%. In 1983 and 1984, contributions and income resumed a similar path of change. Then, as income fell once again in 1985, contributions did not decline but began the slowdown that carried into 1986.

The Conference Board Annual Survey reflects a similar pattern among corporations that have participated in the survey in consecutive years. Each survey year, the responses of a core group of companies are matched with their responses from the previous year to compare changes on a case-by-case basis. Among the matched-sample companies, as in the broader population, increases began to slow in 1985 and have continued to do so with even smaller increases in 1986. Charitable contributions by matched-sample companies grew a slim 1% (in real terms) from 1985 to 1986. (See Chart 11 on page 17 for a graphic representation of the changes in income and contributions in the matched-sample companies.)

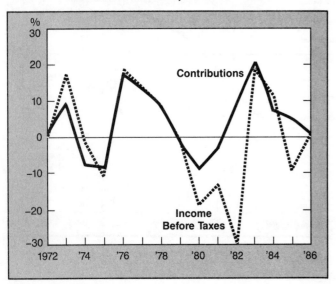

Chart 2:
**Percentage Change in Contributions and Corporate Income Before Taxes in Constant Dollars, 1972 to 1986**

## The Outlook for Corporate Contributions

Corporate contributions will continue to grow but at a very slow pace. Respondents to the 1986 Annual Survey estimated their final 1987 contributions budgets and, as in 1985, reported conservative totals that result in an overall drop of 3% in projected 1987 contributions for the survey sample. About 60% of them expected their 1987 budgets either to remain level or to increase over 1986 levels. Of those anticipating increases, about 45% projected contributions to rise by at least 10%. It is more likely that these increases will offset the effects of the predicted declines, so that the growth of contributions in the aggregate will be flat. Contributions executives who manage the largest programs, and those from petroleum and gas, fabricated metals, and chemical firms, were the most pessimistic respondents. (See Chart 3 on page 3 and Tables 1 and 2 on page 7.)

Although the October 1987 stock market crash probably occurred too late in the year to affect 1987 corporate contributions expenditures, it is likely to have some influence on 1988 giving levels. If economic growth slows in 1988, as has been predicted in the wake of the crash, contributions budgets are likely to follow the downward income trend, but it is not clear how closely.

## Cash and Noncash Giving

Cash contributions grew by about 5% between 1985 and 1986 and represented 79% of all corporate giving by survey participants. The median value of cash donations was $1.2 million, a 9% increase over the 1985 median. The top-ranked company for cash donations gave $77.5 million; and 36 companies made cash contributions of over $10 million each.

Noncash contributions—gifts of securities, company product, property, and equipment—appear to have become firmly established among corporate givers, particularly among manufacturing firms. For the third consecutive year, noncash gifts accounted for one-fifth of total corporate contributions (see Chart 5 on page 4).

Noncash giving has clearly had an impact on the contributions programs of the largest donors (see Table 3 on pages 8-9). Among the top 25 donors, noncash gifts accounted for 30% of total contributions; 12 of the top 75 companies gave well over 50% of their donations in product or property form. Fewer than half of the top 75 (32 firms) gave 100% cash.

Product gifts, at 12% of all donations in 1986, are the largest category of noncash contributions. A total of 69 companies reported product donations of over $200 million in 1986. They form a particularly important part of the contributions programs in several manufacturing industries (see Table 4 on page 10). Sizable amounts of product were donated by electrical machinery and equipment manufacturers ($105 million), food, beverage and tobacco companies ($37 million), chemical companies ($26 million), pharmaceutical companies ($14 million), telecommunications firms ($11 million), and printing and publishing companies ($8 million).

Among the matched-sample companies, gifts of company product increased about 6% between 1985 and 1986, growing slightly faster than cash donations. The largest donation by a single company amounted to $32 million, and 29 companies each made product donations valued at more than $1 million. The median gift of product was $369,000 in 1986, an increase of 85% over the previous year.

Property and equipment donations accounted for about 8% of 1986 contributions, continuing a slide from a high of over 11% in 1984. Among the matched-sample companies, the total dollar value of property and equipment donations dropped over 9% between 1985 and 1986. Most of the gifts in this category are land and buildings, which are not as consistent an element in an individual company's contributions program as gifts of product. Gifts of property are thus not strongly associated with any particular industry and can cause sizable fluctuations in an industry's total contributions from year to year.

In 1986, major gifts of property were made by the food, beverage, and tobacco industry ($49 million), transportation equipment manufacturers ($34 million), insurance companies ($19 million), and chemical companies ($10 million). The largest gift of property reported by a single company was valued at $40 million. The median gift was $123,000, compared to a median of $107,000 in 1985.

Gifts of securities amounted to less than 1% of total contributions for surveyed companies in 1986. A total of $8 million was reported by 12 companies, with a median of $254,000. Securities were mainly given by companies in the service sector, particularly banks, insurance companies, and utilities.

Chart 3:
## Anticipated Changes in 1987 Budgets, by Industry

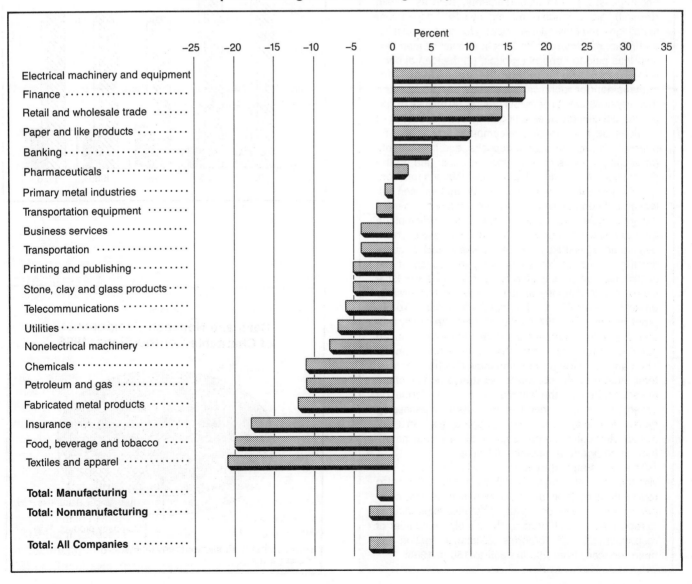

## Corporate Assistance Expenditures

Corporations provide nonprofit groups with types of assistance that are not considered charitable contributions but business expenses. Since 1982, The Conference Board has attempted to quantify this assistance, which is similar in purpose to that of charitable donations—the support of "social, charitable, and other groups to promote the well-being of society." A breakdown of the expenditures that meet The Conference Board's definition of corporate assistance appears in the box below.

Taken together, corporate assistance outlays and charitable contributions constitute a company's total social investment. Corporate assistance represented approximately 20% of that total between 1982 and 1986. The aggregate ratio of corporate assistance expenditures to charitable contributions has fluctuated somewhat over that five-year period (see Chart 7 on page 6).

In comparison to charitable contributions, corporate assistance expenditures among matched-case companies grew strongly in 1986, registering a 24% increase in aggregate ex-

---

### Defining Corporate Assistance

In 1982, five major categories of expenditures to nonprofit groups, plus a sixth category covering administrative costs, were defined by The Conference Board as "corporate assistance expenditures." The six categories encompass: (1) cash disbursements, such as "basic research" grants made by a company's R&D department to colleges and universities; support for public television and radio; monies paid for benefit events; or membership fees paid to nonprofit groups; (2) the loan of company personnel to nonprofit organizations for management or technical assistance; (3) product and property donations to nonprofit groups; (4) the use of corporate facilities (such as office or meeting space) or of services (such as printing or computer processing) by nonprofit groups; (5) loans, deposits, and investments for social purposes at below-market rates; and (6) the direct costs of administering the contributions function.

In the years that The Conference Board has been collecting data on corporate assistance, many companies did not complete the corporate assistance portion of the questionnaire either because they did not make such expenditures or because they were unable to track or quantify them. One problem has been that much of the assistance is in noncash forms, such as the use of facilities or loan of company personnel, and is not necessarily under the control of the contributions function. To improve reporting, in 1987, for the first time, the survey section relating to corporate assistance was sent to a limited panel of companies, rather than to the whole sample. The panel is made up of companies that have consistently answered the corporate assistance section of the questionnaire over the last four years. The information collected over that period has been useful in assessing general trends and priorities in corporate assistance activities, although not representative of the actual magnitude of corporate assistance activities.

The data supplied by the panel will continue to provide the trend information available in the past. It will also reduce the complexity of the questionnaire for those companies that have no corporate assistance expenditures to report. As a result of using the panel, the number of respondents to the corporate assistance section has been reduced, from 280 in 1985 to 150 in 1986.

---

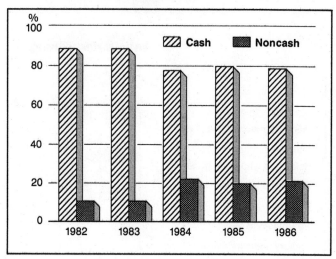

Chart 4:
### Cash and Noncash Giving 1982-1986

---

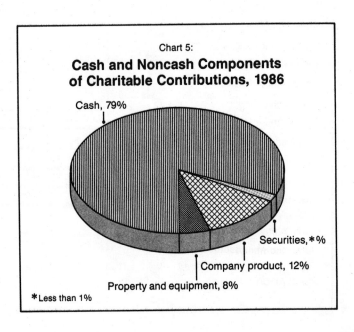

Chart 5:
### Cash and Noncash Components of Charitable Contributions, 1986

Cash, 79%

Securities, *%

Company product, 12%

Property and equipment, 8%

*Less than 1%

Chart 6:
# Cash and Noncash Contributions by Industry, 1986

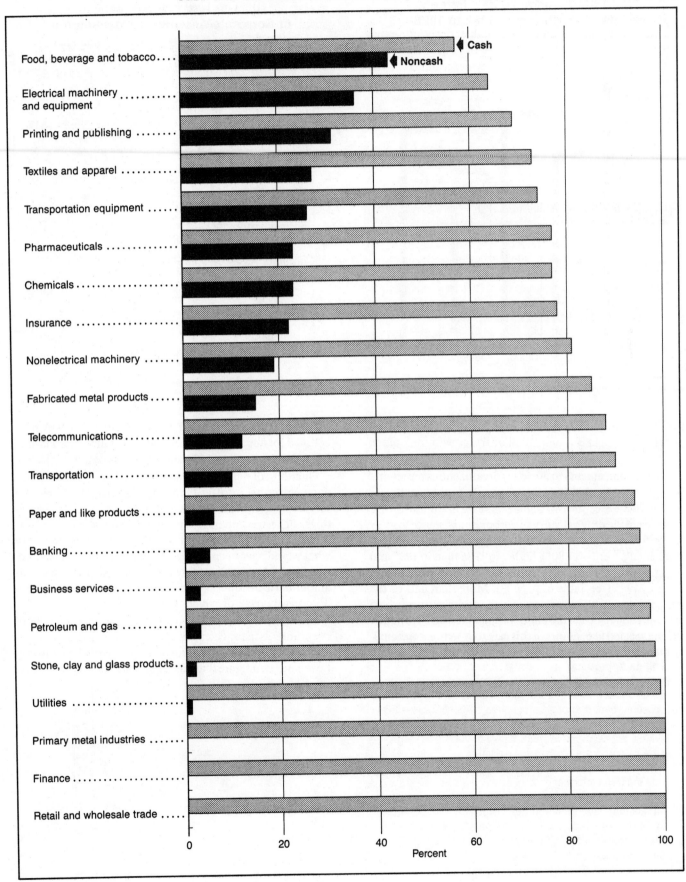

Food, beverage and tobacco....

Electrical machinery ...........
and equipment

Printing and publishing .......

Textiles and apparel ...........

Transportation equipment ......

Pharmaceuticals ..............

Chemicals .................

Insurance .................

Nonelectrical machinery .......

Fabricated metal products .....

Telecommunications ..........

Transportation ...............

Paper and like products .......

Banking .....................

Business services ............

Petroleum and gas ...........

Stone, clay and glass products..

Utilities ....................

Primary metal industries .......

Finance ...................

Retail and wholesale trade .....

Percent

**Corporate Assistance as a Percent
of Total Contributions, 1982 to 1986**

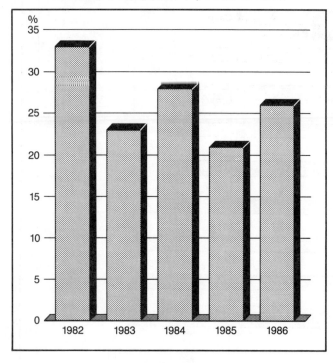

**The Top Five Industry Leaders
in Corporate Assistance Expenditures**

*Total Corporate Assistance Expenditures ($ Millions)*

| | |
|---|---|
| Electrical machinery and equipment | $65 |
| Chemicals | $55 |
| Pharmaceuticals | $23 |
| Food, beverage, and tobacco | $20 |
| Insurance | $17 |

*Median Corporate Assistance Expenditures
($ Thousands)*

| | |
|---|---|
| Electrical machinery and equipment | $3,055 |
| Chemicals | $1,991 |
| Pharmaceuticals | $1,356 |
| Petroleum and gas | $1,202 |
| Textiles and apparel | $ 998 |

*Corporate Assistance as Percent of Total
Contributions*

| | |
|---|---|
| Utilities | 55% |
| Chemicals | 55% |
| Paper and like products | 49% |
| Pharmaceuticals | 42% |
| Electrical machinery and equipment | 30% |

penditures and a 16% increase in the median value of corporate assistance. But almost all of the growth took place in one category—cash disbursements.

Cash disbursements to 501(c)(3) organizations represented the largest category of corporate assistance expenditures and, with the exception of a small increase in administrative costs, were the *only* category of corporate assistance to grow in 1986. Among matched-case companies, total cash disbursements were over 80% higher in 1986 than in 1985 and accounted for 57% of all corporate assistance, compared to 39% in 1985 (see Table 6, page 11). More than half of the cash disbursements were research grants to universities, which have historically been the major recipients of cash corporate assistance; in 1986, grants in this category were exceptionally high, with a median of $500,000, double the 1985 median (see Table 7, page 11).

One-third of the companies reporting corporate assistance activities make product and property donations, which accounted for about 15% of corporate assistance expenditures. Most donations, about $24 million, were company product.

One-third of reporting companies also make loans of company personnel or offer the use of company facilities and services to nonprofit groups as part of their social expenditures. Fifteen companies reported making loans, deposits, or investments for social purposes at rates of return below what would have been applied on a regular market transaction. The value of the income foregone by such transactions amounted to $6 million, and the face value totaled $106 million, nearly 85% of which was in loans.

Administrative expenses accounted for another 12% of corporate assistance expenditures. Administrative costs represent a median of approximately 5% of the contributions budget, a figure that has remained relatively stable over the last five years (see Table 9, page 12).

## Table 1: Actual and Anticipated Changes in Contributions Budgets, 1985-1987
by Industry

| Industry Classification | Number of Companies | 1985-1986 Actual Percentage Change | 1986-1987 Anticipated Percentage Change |
|---|---|---|---|
| Chemicals | 25 | 2% | −11% |
| Electrical machinery and equipment | 21 | 11 | 31%a |
| Fabricated metals | 6 | 16 | −12 |
| Food, beverage and tobacco | 15 | 56%a | −20%a |
| Machinery, nonelectrical | 15 | − 5 | − 8 |
| Paper and like products | 9 | − 5 | 10 |
| Petroleum and gas[1] | 20 | −19 | −11 |
| Pharmaceuticals | 9 | − 1 | 2 |
| Primary metal industries | 9 | −15 | − 1 |
| Printing and publishing | 6 | 64%a | − 5 |
| Stone, clay and glass | 5 | − 9 | − 5 |
| Textiles and apparel | 2 | * | * |
| Transportation equipment[2] | 11 | − 9 | − 2 |
| Total: Manufacturing | 153 | 2% | − 2% |
| Banking | 37 | 16 | 5 |
| Business services[3] | 6 | 0 | − 4 |
| Finance | 3 | * | * |
| Insurance | 31 | −16%a | −18%a |
| Retail and wholesale trade | 10 | 2 | 14 |
| Telecommunications | 8 | 27 | − 6 |
| Transportation | 4 | * | * |
| Utilities | 40 | 15 | − 7 |
| Total: Nonmanufacturing | 139 | 6% | − 3% |
| Total: All Companies | 292 | 3% | − 3% |

[1]Includes mining companies.
[2]Includes tire manufacturers.
[3]Includes engineering and construction companies.
*Total include all cases, but details omit industries with fewer than 5 cases.

[a] These large changes reflect the effects of extraordinary noncash contributions.

## Table 2: Anticipated Changes in Contributions Budget, 1987
By Size of Program

| Program Size | Number of Companies | Median Percentage Increase 1986-1987 | Aggregate Percentage Increase 1986-1987 |
|---|---|---|---|
| Less than $500,000 | 73 | 2.1% | 0.7% |
| $500,000 to $1 million | 57 | 3.0 | 4.3 |
| $1 million to $5 million | 118 | 3.2 | 0.0 |
| $5 million and over | 81 | 2.2 | −3.7 |
| Total | 329 | 2.8% | −2.7% |

# Table 3: Cash and Noncash Charitable Contributions of 75 Largest Donors, 1986

| Company Rank | Total Contributions (dollars) | Cash | Cash as % Of Total | Securities | Securities as % Of Total | Company Product | Company Product as % Of Total | Property & Equipment | Property & Equipment as % Of Total |
|---|---|---|---|---|---|---|---|---|---|
| 1 | $111,900,000 | $77,500,000 | 69% | $0 | 0% | $32,000,000 | 29% | $ 2,400,000 | 2% |
| 2 | 72,076,000 | 23,642,000 | 33 | 0 | 0 | 8,344,000 | 12 | 40,090,000 | 56 |
| 3 | 56,115,192 | 33,524,775 | 60 | 0 | 0 | 0 | 0 | 22,590,417 | 40 |
| 4 | 46,563,622 | 36,154,482 | 78 | 0 | 0 | 10,409,140 | 22 | 0 | 0 |
| 5 | 46,099,967 | 45,684,915 | 99 | 0 | 0 | 0 | 0 | 415,052 | 1 |
| 6 | 34,973,597 | 30,195,821 | 86 | 0 | 0 | 4,777,776 | 14 | 0 | 0 |
| 7 | 32,949,125 | 5,755,125 | 17 | 0 | 0 | 27,194,000 | 83 | 0 | 0 |
| 8 | 30,900,000 | 21,573,000 | 70 | 0 | 0 | 300,000 | 1 | 9,027,000 | 29 |
| 9 | 29,747,359 | 11,673,359 | 39 | 0 | 0 | 0 | 0 | 18,074,000 | 61 |
| 10 | 26,141,026 | 21,293,977 | 81 | 0 | 0 | 0 | 0 | 4,847,049 | 19 |
| 11 | 25,830,431 | 25,702,686 | 100 | 0 | 0 | 8,210 | * | 119,535 | * |
| 12 | 24,940,506 | 24,940,506 | 100 | 0 | 0 | 0 | 0 | 0 | 0 |
| 13 | 23,886,000 | 12,215,000 | 51 | 0 | 0 | 7,771,000 | 33 | 3,900,000 | 16 |
| 14 | 21,700,000 | 11,500,000 | 53 | 0 | 0 | 10,200,000 | 47 | 0 | 0 |
| 15 | 21,306,000 | 15,493,000 | 73 | 0 | 0 | 5,813,000 | 27 | 0 | 0 |
| 16 | 20,781,538 | 20,781,538 | 100 | 0 | 0 | 0 | 0 | 0 | 0 |
| 17 | 19,750,222 | 19,750,222 | 100 | 0 | 0 | 0 | 0 | 0 | 0 |
| 18 | 19,154,503 | 19,154,503 | 100 | 0 | 0 | 0 | 0 | 0 | 0 |
| 19 | 17,883,448 | 17,883,448 | 100 | 0 | 0 | 0 | 0 | 0 | 0 |
| 20 | 17,654,000 | 17,630,000 | 100 | 0 | 0 | 0 | 0 | 24,000 | * |
| 21 | 17,566,562 | 10,935,030 | 62 | 0 | 0 | 6,631,532 | 38 | 0 | 0 |
| 22 | 17,263,356 | 4,263,356 | 25 | 0 | 0 | 13,000,000 | 75 | 0 | 0 |
| 23 | 15,146,933 | 3,852,915 | 25 | 0 | 0 | 11,294,018 | 75 | 0 | 0 |
| 24 | 14,750,000 | 12,148,186 | 82 | 0 | 0 | 0 | 0 | 2,601,814 | 18 |
| 25 | 14,631,404 | 14,242,388 | 97 | 0 | 0 | 167,168 | 1 | 221,848 | 2 |
| 26 | 14,297,171 | 14,297,171 | 100 | 0 | 0 | 0 | 0 | 0 | 0 |
| 27 | 13,290,510 | 4,862,994 | 37 | 0 | 0 | 8,427,516 | 63 | 0 | 0 |
| 28 | 13,006,438 | 13,006,438 | 100 | 0 | 0 | 0 | 0 | 0 | 0 |
| 29 | 12,868,199 | 4,103,750 | 32 | 0 | 0 | 0 | 0 | 8,764,449 | 68 |
| 30 | 12,377,815 | 12,377,815 | 100 | 0 | 0 | 0 | 0 | 0 | 0 |
| 31 | 12,337,985 | 12,337,985 | 100 | 0 | 0 | 0 | 0 | 0 | 0 |
| 32 | 12,000,000 | 12,000,000 | 100 | 0 | 0 | 0 | 0 | 0 | 0 |
| 33 | 11,952,682 | 1,515,667 | 13 | 0 | 0 | 2,437,015 | 20 | 8,000,000 | 67 |
| 34 | 11,647,000 | 11,397,000 | 98 | 0 | 0 | 250,000 | 2 | 0 | 0 |
| 35 | 10,768,448 | 10,293,221 | 96 | 0 | 0 | 0 | 0 | 475,227 | 4 |
| 36 | 10,746,200 | 8,646,200 | 80 | 0 | 0 | 2,100,000 | 20 | 0 | 0 |
| 37 | 10,487,160 | 10,441,250 | 100 | 0 | 0 | 0 | 0 | 45,910 | * |
| 38 | 10,480,308 | 10,480,308 | 100 | 0 | 0 | 0 | 0 | 0 | 0 |
| 39 | 10,478,548 | 10,478,548 | 100 | 0 | 0 | 0 | 0 | 0 | 0 |
| 40 | 10,427,982 | 10,383,474 | 100 | 0 | 0 | 0 | 0 | 44,508 | * |
| 41 | 10,352,585 | 10,352,585 | 100 | 0 | 0 | 0 | 0 | 0 | 0 |
| 42 | 10,259,781 | 10,259,781 | 100 | 0 | 0 | 0 | 0 | 0 | 0 |
| 43 | 10,051,138 | 10,051,138 | 100 | 0 | 0 | 0 | 0 | 0 | 0 |
| 44 | 9,803,589 | 9,803,589 | 100 | 0 | 0 | 0 | 0 | 0 | 0 |
| 45 | 9,642,457 | 9,641,166 | 100 | 0 | 0 | 0 | 0 | 1,291 | * |
| 46 | 9,583,000 | 9,583,000 | 100 | 0 | 0 | 0 | 0 | 0 | 0 |
| 47 | 9,466,526 | 2,177,929 | 23 | 0 | 0 | 7,288,597 | 77 | 0 | 0 |
| 48 | 9,438,352 | 9,438,352 | 100 | 0 | 0 | 0 | 0 | 0 | 0 |
| 49 | 9,381,957 | 8,587,770 | 92 | 0 | 0 | 0 | 0 | 794,187 | 8 |
| 50 | 8,874,673 | 648,790 | 7 | 0 | 0 | 8,225,883 | 93 | 0 | 0 |

Details in each row may not add to 100 percent due to rounding.

n.a. = Not available.

*Less than 1 percent.

## Table 3: Cash and Noncash Charitable Contributions of 75 Largest Donors, 1986 (continued)

| Company Rank | Total Contributions (dollars) | Cash | Cash as % Of Total | Securities | Securities as % Of Total | Company Product | Company Product as % Of Total | Property & Equipment | Property & Equipment as % Of Total |
|---|---|---|---|---|---|---|---|---|---|
| 51 | 8,697,524 | 6,723,642 | 77 | 0 | 0 | 1,973,882 | 23 | 0 | 0 |
| 52 | 8,570,204 | 7,789,771 | 91 | 0 | 0 | 0 | 0 | 780,433 | 9 |
| 53 | 8,425,955 | 8,425,955 | 100 | 0 | 0 | 0 | 0 | 0 | 0 |
| 54 | 8,306,909 | 8,306,909 | 100 | 0 | 0 | 0 | 0 | 0 | 0 |
| 55 | 8,262,778 | 8,262,778 | 100 | 0 | 0 | 0 | 0 | 0 | 0 |
| 56 | 8,107,494 | 8,107,494 | 100 | 0 | 0 | 0 | 0 | 0 | 0 |
| 57 | 7,935,225 | 5,456,331 | 69 | 0 | 0 | 2,313,957 | 29 | 164,937 | 2 |
| 58 | 7,867,459 | 7,563,817 | 96 | 0 | 0 | 60,442 | 1 | 243,200 | 3 |
| 59 | 7,695,000 | 7,695,000 | 100 | 0 | 0 | 0 | 0 | 0 | 0 |
| 60 | 7,687,473 | 6,909,426 | 90 | 0 | 0 | 778,047 | 10 | 0 | 0 |
| 61 | 7,659,849 | 7,659,849 | 100 | 0 | 0 | 0 | 0 | 0 | 0 |
| 62 | 7,568,820 | 3,438,820 | 45 | 0 | 0 | 4,130,000 | 55 | 0 | 0 |
| 63 | 7,533,880 | 7,177,572 | 95 | 0 | 0 | 356,308 | 5 | 0 | 0 |
| 64 | 7,461,431 | 7,461,431 | 100 | 0 | 0 | 0 | 0 | 0 | 0 |
| 65 | 7,386,522 | 7,086,522 | 96 | 0 | 0 | 0 | 0 | 300,000 | 4 |
| 66 | 7,363,023 | 7,363,023 | 100 | 0 | 0 | 0 | 0 | 0 | 0 |
| 67 | 7,278,297 | 7,278,297 | 100 | 0 | 0 | 0 | 0 | 0 | 0 |
| 68 | 7,163,541 | 2,763,541 | 39 | 0 | 0 | 4,400,000 | 61 | 0 | 0 |
| 69 | 6,971,414 | 6,971,414 | 100 | 0 | 0 | 0 | 0 | 0 | 0 |
| 70 | 6,945,000 | 5,860,000 | 84 | 0 | 0 | 1,085,000 | 16 | 0 | 0 |
| 71 | 6,615,481 | 5,865,481 | 89 | 0 | 0 | 0 | 0 | 750,000 | 11 |
| 72 | 6,599,806 | 6,599,806 | 100 | 0 | 0 | 0 | 0 | 0 | 0 |
| 73 | 6,531,007 | 6,531,007 | 100 | 0 | 0 | 0 | 0 | 0 | 0 |
| 74 | 6,267,193 | 3,491,409 | 56 | 0 | 0 | 0 | 0 | 2,775,784 | 44 |
| 75 | 6,003,720 | 6,003,720 | 100 | 0 | 0 | 0 | 0 | 0 | 0 |
| Total | $1,240,636,300 | $931,449,168 | 75% | 0 | 0 | $181,736,491 | 15% | $127,450,641 | 10% |

**Table 4: Cash and Noncash Charitable Contributions 1986—**
Companies Grouped by Industry Classification (with at least 5 cases in each)[a]

| Industry Classification | Number of Companies | Total Contributions Cash and Noncash ($ Thousands) | Cash as a Percent of Total Contributions | Securities as a Percent of Total Contributions | Company Product as a Percent of Total Contributions | Property and Equipment as a Percent of Total Contributions |
|---|---|---|---|---|---|---|
| Chemicals | 26 | $ 154,365 | 77% | 0 | 17% | 6% |
| Electrical machinery and equipment | 29 | 301,416 | 64 | 0 | 35 | 1 |
| Fabricated metals | 6 | 4,794 | 85 | 0 | 16 | 0 |
| Food, beverage and tobacco | 24 | 198,909 | 57 | 0 | 19 | 25 |
| Machinery, nonelectrical | 15 | 24,859 | 81 | 0 | 6 | 13 |
| Paper and like products | 11 | 18,818 | 94 | 0 | 3 | 3 |
| Petroleum and gas[1] | 24 | 231,611 | 97 | 0 | 0 | 3 |
| Pharmaceuticals | 10 | 76,213 | 77 | 0 | 18 | 5 |
| Primary metal | 11 | 16,393 | 99 | 0 | 0 | 0 |
| Printing and publishing | 9 | 27,378 | 69 | 0 | 30 | 2 |
| Stone, clay and glass | 6 | 8,484 | 98 | 0 | 1 | 0 |
| Textiles and apparel | 6 | 6,399 | 73 | 0 | 3 | 24 |
| Transportation equipment[2] | 11 | 134,105 | 74 | 0 | 0 | 25 |
| Total: Manufacturing | 188 | $1,203,744 | 75% | 0 | 16% | 9% |
| Banking | 47 | 105,068 | 95 | 4 | 0 | 1 |
| Business services[3] | 8 | 10,705 | 97 | 0 | 0 | 3 |
| Finance | 5 | 10,345 | 100 | 0 | 0 | 0 |
| Insurance | 43 | 103,444 | 78 | 4 | 0 | 18 |
| Retail and wholesale trade | 13 | 63,120 | 100 | 0 | 0 | 0 |
| Telecommunications | 13 | 116,079 | 88 | 0 | 9 | 3 |
| Transportation | 5 | 6,855 | 90 | 0 | 0 | 10 |
| Utilities | 42 | 49,115 | 99 | 1 | 0 | 1 |
| Total: Nonmanufacturing | 175 | 464,731 | 91% | 2% | 2% | 5% |
| Total: All Companies | 363 | $1,668,475 | 79% | * | 12% | 8% |

[1]Includes mining companies.
[2]Includes tire manufacturers.
[3]Includes engineering and construction companies.
*Less than 1 percent.
[a]Total for an industry may not add to 100 percent because of rounding.

**Table 5: Comparison of Charitable Contributions Expenditures, 1985 and 1986**
310 Matched Companies

| | 1985 Foundation Program | | 1985 Direct Giving Program | | Total | | 1986 Foundation Program | | 1986 Direct Giving Program | | Total | |
|---|---|---|---|---|---|---|---|---|---|---|---|---|
| | Sum | Percent | Sum | Percent | Sum | Percent | Sum | Percent | Sum | Percent | Sum | Percent |
| Cash | $553,661 | 99.8% | $591,213 | 65.3% | $1,144,874 | 78.4% | $567,143 | 99.9% | $629,527 | 66.1% | $1,196,670 | 78.7% |
| Securities | 275 | .0 | 4,165 | 0.5 | 4,440 | 0.3 | — | 0.0 | 7,830 | 0.8 | 7,830 | 0.5 |
| Product | 283 | 0.1 | 171,951 | 19.0 | 172,234 | 11.8 | 8 | .0 | 190,358 | 20.0 | 190,366 | 12.5 |
| Property and equipment | 391 | 0.1 | 137,542 | 15.2 | 137,933 | 9.5 | 512 | 0.1 | 124,573 | 13.1 | 125,085 | 8.2 |
| Total [a] | $554,610 | 100.0% | $904,871 | 100.0% | $1,459,481 | 100.0% | $567,663 | 100.0% | $952,288 | 100.0% | $1,519,951 | 100.0% |

[a]Details may not add to totals due to rounding.

## Table 6: Comparison of Corporate Assistance Expenditures—Matched Cases, 1986-1985

| Description | Number of Companies | Sum ($000) 1986 | Sum ($000) 1985 | % Change | Median 1986 | Median 1985 |
|---|---|---|---|---|---|---|
| Cash Disbursements to 501(C) (3) Organizations Not Reported as Charitable Contributions . . . . | 108 | $128,112 | $ 69,620 | 84% | $ 97,576 | $ 85,635 |
| Loan of Company Personnel . . . . . . . . . . . . . . . | 44 | 16,845 | 17,654 | – 5 | 35,021 | 33,000 |
| Donations of Product and Property Not Reported as Charitable Contributions . . . . . . . | 48 | 35,639 | 45,664 | –22 | 28,050 | 25,033 |
| Use of Corporate Facilities or Services . . . . . . . . | 40 | 11,183 | 13,578 | –18 | 20,537 | 25,216 |
| Loans at Below-Market Yields . . . . . . . . . . . . . . | 15 | 5,902 | 7,357 | –20 | 40,000 | 122,000 |
| Administrative Cost for Contributions Function . . | 95 | 27,002 | 26,845 | 1 | 135,000 | 99,993 |
| Total . . . . . . . . . . . . . . . . . . . . . . . . . . . . . | 142 | $224,683 | $180,718 | 24% | $221,019 | $190,046 |

## Table 7: Corporate Assistance—Cash Disbursements to 501(c)(3) Organizations

| Category of Disbursement | Number of Companies | Total Dollar Value ($ Thousands) | Percent of Total Cash Disbursements | Percent of Total Corporate Assistance | Median Dollar Value |
|---|---|---|---|---|---|
| "Basic research" grants . . . . . . . . . . . . . | 35 | $ 77,744 | 57% | 37% | $500,000 |
| Other college grants . . . . . . . . . . . . . . . | 20 | 3,517 | 3 | 2 | 41,250 |
| Public TV and radio . . . . . . . . . . . . . . . . | 25 | 552 | * | * | 7,000 |
| Benefit events . . . . . . . . . . . . . . . . . . . | 68 | 6,978 | 5 | 3 | 40,950 |
| Other grants . . . . . . . . . . . . . . . . . . . . . | 78 | 29,625 | 22 | 14 | 39,622 |
| Unspecified . . . . . . . . . . . . . . . . . . . . . . | 5 | 17,286 | 13 | 8 | — |
| Total . . . . . . . . . . . . . . . . . . . . . | 113 | $135,703 | 100% | 64% | $115,085 |

* Less than 1%

## Table 8: Corporate Assistance Expenditures, 1986
Companies Grouped by Industry Classification

| | | Sums | | Medians | |
|---|---|---|---|---|---|
| Industry Classification | Number of Companies | Total Corporate Assistance ($000) | Corporate Assistance as Percent of Total Contributions* | Total Corporate Assistance ($000) | Corporate Assistance as Percent of Total Contributions* |
| Chemicals | 11 | $ 54,866 | 55% | $1,991 | 37% |
| Electrical machinery and equipment | 11 | 64,733 | 30 | 3,055 | 21 |
| Food, beverage and tobacco | 9 | 19,523 | 15 | 296 | 10 |
| Machinery, nonelectrical | 9 | 2,432 | 15 | 85 | 4 |
| Paper and like products | 4 | 2,946 | * | * | * |
| Petroleum and gas[1] | 8 | 13,840 | 14 | 1,202 | 8 |
| Pharmaceuticals | 6 | 22,800 | 42 | 1,356 | 10 |
| Primary metals | 3 | 1,641 | * | * | * |
| Printing and publishing | 4 | 561 | * | * | * |
| Stone, clay and glass | 4 | 629 | * | * | * |
| Textiles and apparel | 1 | 998 | * | * | * |
| Total: Manufacturing | 70 | $184,968 | 28% | $ 560 | 10% |
| Banking | 20 | 11,842 | 17 | 144 | 13 |
| Business services[2] | 5 | 781 | 11 | 60 | 11 |
| Finance | 2 | 95 | * | * | * |
| Insurance | 25 | 16,668 | 20 | 126 | 15 |
| Retail and wholesale trade | 4 | 2,517 | * | * | * |
| Telecommunications | 5 | 2,607 | 11 | 415 | 9 |
| Transportation | 2 | 81 | * | * | * |
| Utilities | 17 | 14,097 | 55 | 78 | 14 |
| Total: Nonmanufacturing | 80 | $ 48,688 | 20% | $ 136 | 12% |
| Total: All Companies | 150 | $233,656 | 26% | $ 232 | 11% |

[1]Includes mining companies.
[2]Includes engineering and construction companies.
*Totals include all cases, but details omit industries with fewer than 5 cases.

## Table 9: Administrative Cost as a Percent of Contributions
Medians by Size of Contributions Budget

| Size of Contributions Budget | Number of Companies | Administrative Cost as a Percent of Contributions Budget (Median) |
|---|---|---|
| Under $500,000 | 16 | 5.7% |
| $500,000—$1 million | 9 | 8.2 |
| $1 million—$5 million | 37 | 4.5 |
| Over $5 million | 38 | 3.7 |
| Total | 100 | 4.7% |

Median Value of Administrative Costs: $135,100

# Chapter 2
# Measuring Contributions Activity

Contributions budgets were essentially stable in 1986; there were no extraordinary swings in budget size or in the ratio of contributions to pretax income; it was generally a year of fine-tuning. To assess a company's position among its peers, it is necessary to look at the differences that arise by industry category, income, sales, asset, or employee size. This chapter details the different measures corporate contributions managers use to identify leadership in the contributions field.

The 372 survey participants reported a total of $1.68 billion in corporate contributions—37% of the estimated contributions made by all U.S. corporations. The budgets reported in the survey ranged in size from approximately $100,000 to $112 million, with a median of $1.4 million.

## Foundation Giving

Corporate foundations have multiplied rapidly over the last three years. Between 1984 and 1986, 32 new foundations were established by participants in the Annual Survey. In the last forty years such a flurry of activity among survey respondents has occurred only twice: from 1979 to 1980, when 23 companies set up foundations; and between 1951 and 1953, when 45 firms formed new foundations. Although foundations have traditionally been concentrated among manufacturers, most of those created recently were established by service sector companies (21 out of 32).

As a result of all this activity, the proportion of companies with foundations has climbed from 42% in 1977 to 65% in 1986 (see Table 10 on page 19). The proportion of total contributions accounted for by foundation giving, in contrast, has not kept pace with the increase in foundations. Since 1981, the share of corporate giving provided by foundation donations has been slowly declining, from 42% to 38% (see Chart 8 on page 15).

Of the 240 foundations responding to the 1986 survey, 224 made contributions totalling $641 million. Foundation disbursements ranged from $15,000 to $30 million, with a median dollar value of $989,000—a 24% increase over the 1985 median. By comparison, the median contribution by direct-giving corporate programs was $780,000.

For the first time since 1979, corporate foundations took in more from their parent corporations than they gave out. Chart 9 (on page 15) tracks the relationship of foundation payouts to pay-ins since 1974, when the Annual Survey began. In lean years, when corporate profits are down, corporations have tended to reduce or eliminate grants to their foundations. Foundations have nevertheless maintained the corporation's level of charitable giving by using the foundation assets and earnings. In 1975 and 1982, both recession years, corporate foundations gave out 40% to 50% more than they received from their parent corporations.

When corporate profits are up, as they were in the mid to late 1970s, corporations fund the foundation asset base. In 1986, about one-third (82) of reporting corporations made grants to their foundations that exceeded what the foundations subsequently paid out in contributions. Seventeen corporations made grants of $10 million or more; 11 of those grants were clearly intended to build the foundation corpus.

## Industry Patterns

Manufacturing companies continued to dominate contributions activity in 1986. Although manufacturers reported 53% of domestic pretax income, they were responsible for 76% of all contributions among the 1986 Annual Survey participants. As a group, manufacturers exceed service companies both in the median dollar level of giving—$2.2 million compared to $958,000—and in the median ratio of contributions to domestic pretax income—1.5% compared to .90%. Only 19 of the top 75 survey donors in 1986 came from the service sector. And, despite a 22% drop in pretax income in 1986, contributions by manufacturers in the matched sample still rose by 2%, while nonmanufacturers increased their contributions at about the same rate as profit growth (see Chart 10 on page 16 for the change in contributions and pretax income by industry).

A number of major changes took place in the median dollar level of giving in several industries between 1985 and 1986. On the positive side, median contributions increased 150% among transportation equipment manufacturers to $7.5 million (the highest median in 1986). The median for printing

# Terms and Concepts Used in This Report

Two major formats for reporting contributions are used throughout this report. The first is a ratio, with contributions divided by such characteristics as pretax income and number of employees. The second is a percentage distribution, with contributions dollars apportioned among major beneficiary groups such as health and human services, education, culture and art, civic and community. In order to interpret these data correctly, it is important to understand the following:

## Worldwide and "U.S.-Only" Data

Respondents to the questionnaire were asked to provide both worldwide and "U.S.-only" data on sales, assets, income before taxes, and number of employees. The worldwide data are the figures reported by corporations in their consolidated financial statements. The "U.S.-only" financial data reflect sales, assets and pretax income derived solely from U.S. operations. The employee-size data reflect only those workers employed in the United States. For those companies that are not multinational (about 34 percent of the sample), "worldwide" and "U.S.-only" data are identical.

While the worldwide data are consistent with tabulated statistics on the corporate sector as reported by various U.S. government agencies, it should be noted that there are no comparable "U.S.-only" figures. U.S. data have customarily been included in this series of Conference Board reports, however, in order to facilitate comparison with the contributions figures, which reflect giving only to domestic or U.S.-based beneficiaries. (Overseas giving is discussed on page 18.)

## Contributions

Corporate contributions and gifts reported to the IRS normally include gifts of property as well as gifts of cash, and the survey questionnaire specifically asked respondents to include the dollar value of gifts of property reported as contributions on the company's income tax return. However, there are two major differences between the contributions figures derived from Internal Revenue Service (IRS) sources and those reported in this study. While both sets of figures include direct giving by corporations, the first difference lies in the treatment of dollars going *into* and *out of* corporate foundations within a given year.

The IRS figures reflect dollars given by a corporation to its foundation, while the survey figures reflect dollars donated by corporate foundations to eligible beneficiaries. This is in keeping with study objectives to measure the flow of dollars actually reaching beneficiaries in any calendar year. Dollars given to the foundation are not necessarily expended within the same year. (See page 13.)

The second major difference between the IRS and the survey figures is the fact that the IRS data reflect the total universe of approximately two million corporations that file tax returns, while the survey data are compiled from a sample of these firms that is weighted toward larger companies.

## Corporate Assistance

Corporate-assistance expenditures are six categories of items that are given to assist social, charitable or other groups to promote the well-being of society, but are *not* taken as a charitable deduction by corporations. These include cash grants given to tax-exempt, 501 (c) (3) organizations that are not reported as contributions; loans of company personnel; donations of products, equipment and property charged to business expense; loans, deposits and investments for social purposes at below-market rates of return; loans of company facilities and services at no charge or below cost; and the direct costs the company incurs in administering the contributions function.

## Corporate Social Expenditure

The sum of charitable contributions and corporate-assistance expenditures, appears only in Table 8B. It represents an attempt to estimate a total for social involvement by major corporations.

## Ratios

It is common practice in the contributions field to speak both of the 5-percent limit on giving, and of setting a "5-percent" target. Since 1936, the Internal Revenue Code has allowed corporations to deduct contributions to charitable organizations up to a maximum of 5 percent of the corporation's *taxable* income with a five-year carry forward. Under the Economic Recovery Tax Act of 1981, this limit was raised to 10 percent. Because taxable income is a closely held figure, it is not possible to collect it from corporations for use in this report. Instead, the ratio is calculated on pretax income.

## Major Categories of Organizations

The problem of classifying and defining the five major areas of corporate support and their subcategories is a continuing one. Classification is made on the basis of the major program objective or organizational goal of the *donee* group. The five major categories of organization used in this survey—health and human services, education, culture and the arts, civic and community, and "other"—include all grant formats: matching gifts, operating support, program support, and capital support. (For more detail on categories, see box on page 20.)

and publishing companies nearly doubled, reaching $3.8 million; and the median for fabricated metals companies advanced almost 60% to $718,000. Increases of 20% to 30% occurred in the medians among banks, telecommunications companies, insurance companies, and nonelectrical machinery manufacturers.

In contrast, significant decreases in medians took place among stone, clay and glass companies (down 63%); petroleum and gas companies (down 61%); electrical equipment and machinery (down 37%); and food, beverage, and tobacco companies (down 23%).

In the ten-year period between 1977 and 1986, the median ratio of contributions to domestic pretax income advanced .50%, to 1.17% for all surveyed companies. But the changes were more pronounced in five industries: For petroleum and gas companies the median ratio increased from .39% to 2.60%, primarily because of the drop in oil company profits in 1986; for electrical machinery and equipment manufacturers (.78% to 2.02%); chemical companies (.85% to 2.04%); transportation equipment manufacturers (.51% to 1.69%); and food, beverage, and tobacco companies (.74% to 1.78%).

Three industries had remarkably stable ratios of contributions to domestic pretax income over the 1977-1986 period: Banking and pharmaceuticals have consistently had median ratios in the range of 1.30 to 1.50%; and utilities, for regulatory reasons, have maintained a level of giving of about .30%. The ratio for telecommunications companies has been slowly rising in recent years, from .35% in the late 1970s to .69% in 1986, as the original regional Bell operating companies and AT&T have established foundations and expanded each of their contributions programs in the aftermath of the 1984 divestiture.

## Industry Leaders

*Median Contributions as a Percent of U.S. Pretax Income*

| | |
|---|---|
| Petroleum and gas | 2.60% |
| Chemicals | 2.04 |
| Electrical machinery and equipment | 2.02 |
| Food, beverage, and tobacco | 1.78 |
| Transportation equipment | 1.69 |

*Median Total Contributions ($ Thousands)*

| | |
|---|---|
| Transportation equipment | $7,481 |
| Pharmaceuticals | $5,972 |
| Telecommunications | $5,200 |
| Food, beverage, and tobacco | $4,252 |
| Printing and publishing | $3,783 |

### Companies with Losses in 1986

Thirty-two or nearly 9% of survey participants reported worldwide income losses in 1986, the highest number of firms since 1983. Nearly half of the companies were in the service sector—transportation, insurance, utilities, and banks. One-third of the companies were in the petroleum and gas and primary metals industries.

Despite their losses, these companies made nearly $74 million in charitable contributions. Twelve companies gave over $1 million each, and four of those were among the top 75 donors in 1986. The median gift among the companies reporting losses was $853,000.

As they have in the past, corporate foundations played an important role in 1986 in maintaining the level of giving of

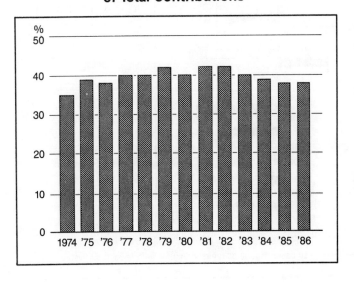

Chart 8:
**Foundation Giving as a Percent of Total Contributions**

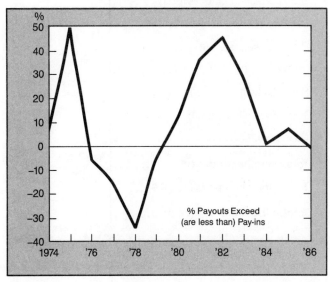

Chart 9:
**Relationship of Foundation Payouts to Pay-ins**

% Payouts Exceed (are less than) Pay-ins

companies experiencing losses. Of the 32 reporting losses, 19 have foundations, which accounted for 84% of the contributions made by their parent companies and paid out over $21 million more than they took in.

### Major Donors

Nearly three-quarters of the total contributions reported in the 1986 Annual Survey were made by 20% of the participants. The top 75 donors listed in Appendix Table 8A (see pages 40-41) gave a total of $1.2 billion, about the same amount given by the leading companies in 1985. The top-ranked company gave $112 million, nearly four times the contributions made by the leading company in 1977 (a 150%

rise when measured in constant 1972 dollars). The median contributions level among the top 75 companies was $10.5 million in 1986, compared to $9.7 million in 1985. More than half of the top companies gave over $10 million each.

Companies with large contributions programs have historically also had high contributions to pretax-income ratios. The median domestic ratio for the top 75 companies rose from 1.76% in 1985 to 2.2% in 1986. The 1986 figure for the entire survey sample was 1.17%. More than half of the top 75 firms reporting U.S. income had contributions ratios of over 2%, and ten companies reported ratios of over 5%. In sharp contrast, ten years earlier, in 1977, only one company reported a ratio of over 2%, and the median domestic ratio for the top 75 companies was only .73%.

Chart 10:

## Percentage Change in Contributions and Worldwide Pretax Income, 1985 and 1986, by Industry

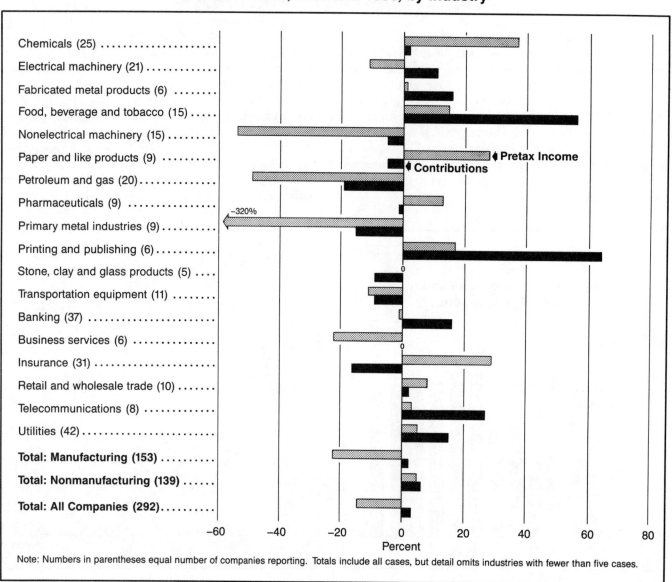

Note: Numbers in parentheses equal number of companies reporting. Totals include all cases, but detail omits industries with fewer than five cases.

Two factors contributed to the relatively high contributions ratios in 1986 among lead companies: Several companies reported considerably lower incomes, and noncash contributions among the top 75 companies was proportionally higher (at 25%) than among the entire sample. (See Table 3 on page 8 for a complete breakdown of the cash and noncash components of the leading companies.)

## 1986 Ratios: Quartiles for Key Groups

Contributions managers have come to rely on the ratio of contributions to pretax income as a useful measure in making comparisons with peer companies. Although the ratio alone cannot completely describe a contributions program, it is important to the planning and budgeting process in contributions management. Appendix Tables 9A through 13B on pages 44-48 present the 25th, 50th, and 75th percentiles for contributions to pretax-income ratios for survey respondents grouped by size of program, income, assets, sales, and industry category.

Historically, larger contributions programs have generally indicated higher contributions to pretax-income ratios, as found in Tables 9A and 9B. In 1986, medians for all but the largest category of program size were lower than in 1985.

The pattern demonstrated in Tables 10A and 10B has been fairly consistent over a ten-year period—as income rises, the ratio of contributions to income tends to decrease, with companies with incomes of $1 billion or more reporting significantly lower ratios than companies in the lowest income categories. In a given year, one income range may have a slightly higher median than the next range down, but on the

whole, the inverse relationship of income to contributions ratio has been a steady one.

In contrast, the relationship of the contributions to income ratio to asset size has not shown a discernible pattern over the years, other than a tendency for ratios to be lower in the middle ranges of assets and somewhat higher at both the high and low ends of the ranges (see Appendix Tables 12A, B).

### Contributions Targets

Setting a goal for contributions as a percent of pretax income continues to be practiced by about 25% of survey participants, most of whom use a ratio based on domestic pretax income as a target (see Table 11 on page 19).

Nearly half of the respondents using the domestic ratio were aiming for 2% or more of pretax income. As in 1985, the majority of respondents (nearly two-thirds) set short-term goals of one to two years in 1986. The remaining third set goals to be met within five years, although one company reported 1999 as the target year.

## Employee Size and Contributions

The ratio of contributions to number of employees has also been a useful benchmark for contributions managers in comparing contributions practices and determining appropriate levels of giving. Since 1981, when The Conference Board first began to report median contributions dollars per employee, the median level has climbed steadily, from $73 per person in 1981 to $164 in 1986 (see Chart 12). The smallest companies (those with under 1,000 employees) have historically made the highest contributions per employee. In 1986, median contributions per employee by these companies were

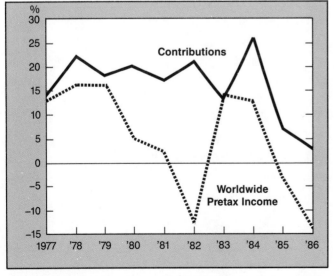

Chart 11:
**Percentage Change in Contributions and Worldwide Pretax Income, 1977 to 1986**

This chart provides contributions in relation to consolidated (worldwide) profits for matched-case companies participating in consecutive survey years.

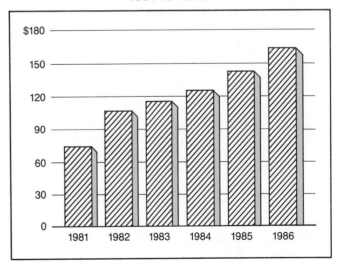

Chart 12:
**Median Contributions per Employee 1981 to 1986**

twice as great as the next highest median (see Chart 13). Medians rose in 1986 for all size categories except for that of 10,000 to 14,999 employees, which dropped about 3 percent.

## Overseas Giving

One-third (123) of the 1986 survey participants made contributions overseas in addition to their domestic giving. Of these companies, 88 reported the dollar value of their overseas contributions, which amounted to $113 million, a modest increase of about 4% over 1985. Overseas donations represented about 12 % of the charitable contributions these companies made in the United States.

The median level of overseas contributions was $120,000, but 19 companies made donations greater than $1 million each, including contributions by one company of $55 million. The electrical machinery and equipment ($64 million) and petroleum and gas ($21 million) industries have historically had major overseas contributions programs. Other industries that reported over $1 million in giving to foreign countries include: chemicals ($6 million), banks ($5 million), food, beverage, and tobacco ($5 million), transportation equipment ($4 million), and pharmaceuticals ($4 million).

Chart 13:
## Contributions per U.S. Employee, 1986
### Medians

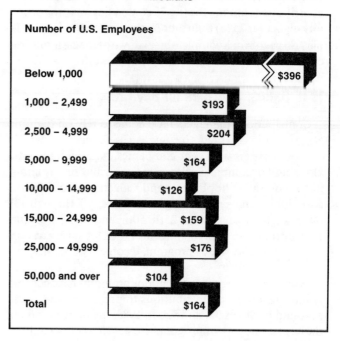

Number of U.S. Employees

| | |
|---|---|
| Below 1,000 | $396 |
| 1,000 – 2,499 | $193 |
| 2,500 – 4,999 | $204 |
| 5,000 – 9,999 | $164 |
| 10,000 – 14,999 | $126 |
| 15,000 – 24,999 | $159 |
| 25,000 – 49,999 | $176 |
| 50,000 and over | $104 |
| Total | $164 |

## Table 10: Concentration of Foundations, by Industry

| Industry Classification | Number of Companies | Number of Foundations | Percent of Companies with Foundations |
|---|---|---|---|
| Chemicals | 28 | 21 | 75% |
| Electrical machinery and equipment | 29 | 21 | 72 |
| Fabricated metals products | 6 | 4 | 67 |
| Food, beverage and tobacco | 24 | 18 | 75 |
| Machinery, nonelectrical | 15 | 13 | 87 |
| Paper and like products | 11 | 10 | 91 |
| Petroleum and gas[1] | 24 | 14 | 58 |
| Pharmaceuticals | 10 | 8 | 80 |
| Primary metals industries | 11 | 10 | 91 |
| Printing and publishing | 10 | 6 | 60 |
| Stone, clay and glass products | 7 | 5 | 71 |
| Textiles and apparel | 6 | 4 | 67 |
| Transportation equipment[2] | 11 | 10 | 91 |
| Total: Manufacturing | 192 | 144 | 75% |
| Banking | 47 | 33 | 70 |
| Business services[3] | 8 | 5 | 63 |
| Finance | 5 | 4 | 80 |
| Insurance | 42 | 27 | 64 |
| Retail and wholesale trade | 15 | 8 | 53 |
| Telecommunications | 13 | 7 | 54 |
| Transportation | 5 | 2 | 40 |
| Utilities | 45 | 10 | 22 |
| Total: Nonmanufacturing | 180 | 96 | 53% |
| Total: All Companies | 372 | 240 | 65% |

[1]Includes mining companies.
[2]Includes tire companies.
[3]Includes engineering and construction companies.

## Table 11: Corporate Targets for 1987 and Beyond
Contributions as a Percent of Pretax Income

| Contributions Targets as a Percent of Pretax Income | U.S. Pretax Income | | Worldwide Pretax Income | |
|---|---|---|---|---|
| | Number | Percent | Number | Percent |
| Less than 1.00% | 11 | 14% | — | — |
| 1.00—1.99% | 30 | 38 | 17 | 65% |
| 2.00—2.99% | 27 | 35 | 6 | 23 |
| 3.00% and over | 10 | 13 | 3 | 12 |
| Total | 78 | 100% | 26 | 100% |

# Definitions of Terms

## The Five Major Categories of Beneficiaries

**Health and Human Services**

Includes support for national health organizations (such as American Cancer Society, Salk Institute, National Homecaring Council, Memorial Sloan-Kettering Cancer Center); national human-services organizations (such as American Red Cross, National Council on Aging, National Committee for Prevention of Child Abuse, Planned Parenthood of America); national youth organizations, (such as Boys Clubs of America); federated drives such as the United Way; support for hospitals; local youth organizations (such as Boys Clubs, Boy and Girl Scouts, YMCA); and other local health and human-service agencies. Among other things, such organizations are concerned with safety, recreation, family planning, drug abuse, and disaster relief.

**Education**

Includes support for institutions of higher education, precollege educational institutions, state and local educational fund-raising groups, economic education groups, and education-related organizations. Program support for research projects funded from the contributions budget is included; however, support of contractual university research is generally excluded.

Educational programs such as employee tuition-refund plans are excluded when funded out of the personnel, public relations, or other expense budgets.

**Culture and the Arts**

Includes visual and performing arts organizations, libraries, museums, cultural centers, arts funds or councils, and the like. Includes support for public radio and television if funded from the contributions budget. Excludes any support funded from expense budgets.

**Civic and Community**

Includes support for national organizations in public-policy research (such as AEI, Brookings, CED); national community improvement (such as Neighborhood Housing Services, Opportunities Industrialization Centers, Local Initiatives Support Corporation, National Urban League, Center for Community Change); national environment and ecology (such as National Wildlife Fund, National Conservation Foundation, Sierra Club); national justice and law organizations (such as Institute for Civil Justice, National Council on Crime and Delinquency, Legal Defense and Education Funds: NOW, MALDEF, Mountain States); other national organizations (such as Independent Sector, National Executive Service Corps, Population Resource Center); municipal or statewide improvement (such as Governors' Task Forces, Planning Associations, Economic Development Council of NYC); local community improvement organizations (such as neighborhood or community-based groups, housing programs, economic development and employment such as PIC's. Job Training Programs); legal systems and services (such as Legal Aid Societies); local environment and ecology (such as zoos, parks, conservation activities); and other local civic and community organizations. Includes local projects such as transportation, housing, law and order, fire prevention, grants to local and state governments, and support of study groups to resolve social problems.

**Other**

Includes support for religious activities, U.S. groups whose principal objective is aid in other countries, (such as CARE, IESC, Council on Foreign Relations), and charitable support for special sports or patriotic events (such as Olympics, Statue of Liberty).

# Chapter 3
# Where the Money Goes

In this era of reassessing and scrutinizing contributions budgets, many companies are taking the opportunity to weigh not only how much they are donating but where. There is a new emphasis on focusing contributions programs to heighten their impact, especially when funds are limited or corporate strategy dictates a closer alignment of contributions program goals and overall corporate objectives.

Internal influences, as well as the external environments in which the corporation operates, exert pressures that shape a company's giving program. As community needs change and are identified, corporate contributions managers must reevaluate the role of the corporation in addressing those needs.

Are corporate priorities shifting? Some significant changes marked the 1986 figures, while some trends continued. As has always been the case, one year alone cannot describe fully what is occurring as the nation's corporate contributions managers sit down to allocate their budgets. But, when placed in the context of five or ten years, some patterns emerge.

Three notable changes took place in 1986 in the allocation of contributions among the five major categories of beneficiaries. (See the box on page 20 for detailed descriptions and examples of organizations in each category.) The greatest change occurred in giving to education. The share of total contributions directed to educational institutions and organizations grew from 38% in 1985 to 43% in 1986, reaching a new height (see Chart 14). Although part of the increase is the result of a $40 million gift of property, when adjusted

Chart 14:
## Distribution of the Contributions Dollar, 1985 and 1986

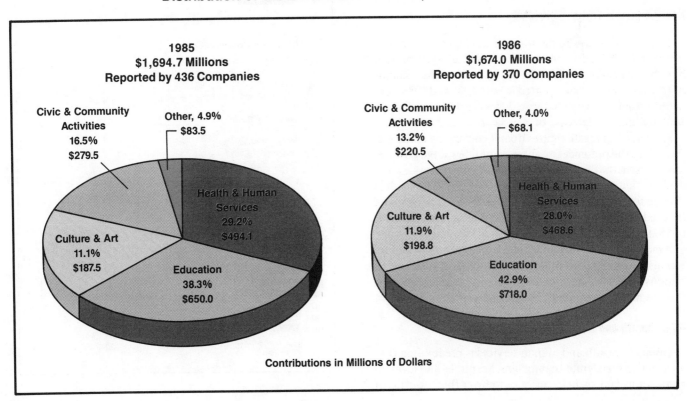

1985
$1,694.7 Millions
Reported by 436 Companies

Civic & Community Activities 16.5% $279.5

Other, 4.9% $83.5

Health & Human Services 29.2% $494.1

Culture & Art 11.1% $187.5

Education 38.3% $650.0

1986
$1,674.0 Millions
Reported by 370 Companies

Civic & Community Activities 13.2% $220.5

Other, 4.0% $68.1

Health & Human Services 28.0% $468.6

Culture & Art 11.9% $198.8

Education 42.9% $718.0

Contributions in Millions of Dollars

for the effect of this one-time gift, the share is 41%—still a major increase and the largest ever reported for education.

The second significant shift in 1986 data is the continuing downturn in donations to civic and community activities, which fell to 13%, down from over 16% in 1985. Part of the explanation for the performance of this category is related to gifts of property. In 1983, after nearly a decade of accounting for 10% to 11% of total giving, donations to civic and community activities leapt to 15% and then to nearly 19% in 1984. The change was mainly due to multimillion dollar property gifts from a handful of companies. In 1985 and 1986, the proportion fell as property gifts became smaller and fewer.

The third important change, though less dramatic than the previous two, nevertheless had social implications. The share of giving to health and human services, after only one year of growth when it reached 29%, fell to 28% in 1986. Since 1975, when health and human services agencies received the major portion of corporate contributions—41%—giving in this category has declined steadily as a share of the total. From 1976 to 1984, nearly all of the loss in share occurred in federated giving—primarily United Way—which decreased from over 22% to approximately 13% of total giving. Over the same period, the proportion of total contributions going to all other health and human services organizations held steady at approximately 17 percent. In 1984, it dropped over 2%, to 14.5%, where it has remained for three years. The increase in share of giving to health and human services that took place in 1985 and the subsequent decrease in 1986 were entirely attributable to federated campaigns.

## Health and Human Services

Total giving to health and human services organizations *decreased* in 1986, not only as a share of total contributions but also in aggregate dollars. Among the matched sample of core companies that reported in both 1985 and 1986, contributions in this category were down nearly $13 million to $401 million—a decrease of 3 percent.

However, aggregate figures do not convey the entire picture, since the presence (or absence) of a few large gifts can misrepresent the practices of the majority of companies. The median figures for 1986 were more positive. The median change for the core companies was an increase of 9%, and the median dollar size of contributions grew from $456,000 to $521,000.

Among all survey respondents, the median dollar amount was also over $500,000 and the median share of total contributions was 38%—both values representing the highest of all the five major categories of beneficiaries.

### Other Health and Human Services Organizations

Giving to health and human services is predominantly a local activity. Federated campaigns, hospitals, and local organizations and agencies account for over three-fourths of

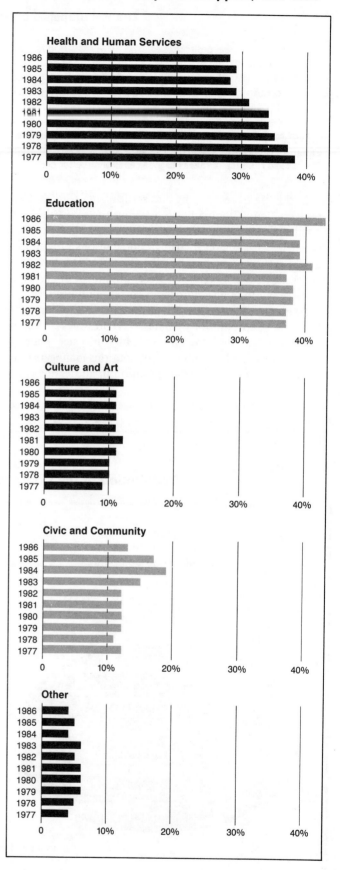

Chart 15:
**Beneficiaries of Corporate Support, 1977-1986**

## The Relationship of Program Size to Priorities

Historically, two strong patterns have emerged in corporate giving that are related to the size of the contributions budget: (1) the smaller the budget, the greater the proportion to health and human services; and (2) the larger the budget, the greater the portion to education.

In general, smaller budgets tend to mean fewer resources of all types—staff, time, and so forth. Without those resources, the individual responsible for contributions decisions may find it extremely difficult either to thoroughly assess community needs or to conduct a rigorous screening process of grant requests. In such situations, it has been more effective to delegate those functions to the United Way or other federated giving programs.

The predominance of educational giving among companies with the largest programs (over $5 million) reflects the industrial composition of this size category. Most of the companies with substantial contributions budgets are in the manufacturing sector—particularly transportation equipment manufacturers, petroleum and gas companies, pharmaceutical companies, and electrical equipment and machinery manufacturers. These industries have a history of major funding of educational programs—especially higher education—because of their critical need for highly trained technical staff.

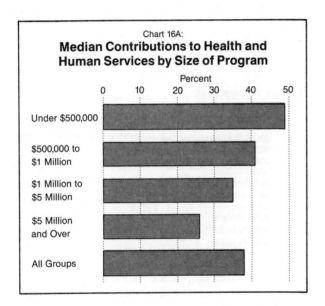

Chart 16A:
**Median Contributions to Health and Human Services by Size of Program**

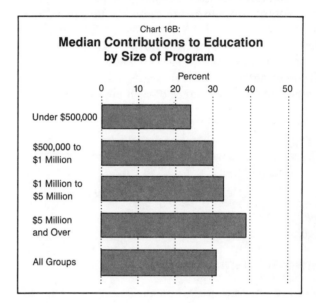

Chart 16B:
**Median Contributions to Education by Size of Program**

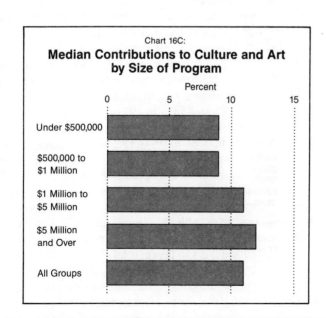

Chart 16C:
**Median Contributions to Culture and Art by Size of Program**

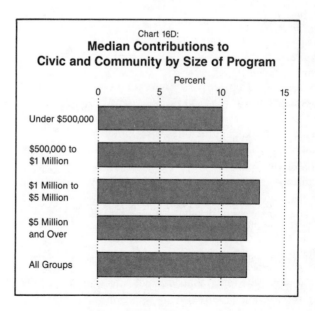

Chart 16D:
**Median Contributions to Civic and Community by Size of Program**

all giving in this category, compared to only 14% for national organizations. Of the remaining 10%, 1% goes to matching gifts and 9% to unspecified beneficiaries. Over the last nine years, however, the proportions of national versus local giving have been very gradually shifting, with national giving climbing from 5% in 1978 to 14% in 1986, while local giving declined from 88% to 65 percent.

Much of the decline in the local portion of health and human services contributions has taken place in giving to hospitals. Since 1980, both the share and the dollars to hospitals have decreased, from $42 million (12%) to $30 million (7%) in 1986, with almost all of the decrease occurring in giving to capital campaigns.

Of the non-federated giving portion of the health and human services budget, giving to human services (including youth programs) at 26% of the total given in this category, exceeds contributions to health causes, at 16% (see Chart 19 on page 27).

Recent research and published articles on critical social issues strongly emphasize the need for intervening in the lives of the disadvantaged at an early age. Advocates of early intervention cite the importance of such programs as nutri-

tion and prenatal care for pregnant teenagers and early childhood education. As the data collected in the Survey are categorized by organization and not by program, it is difficult to clearly identify or to measure the corporate response to this newly articulated need. However, corporate contributions to *organizations* that specifically serve youth have been *declining* as a share of contributions since 1978, when they represented 10% of all health and human services giving, compared to a current 6 percent.

It may be too early to gauge whether corporations will become major supporters of such programs, since most of the new findings did not receive wide coverage in the media or among corporate contributions leaders until 1987. Anecdotal evidence suggests that corporations are recognizing the critical long-term implications of an economically and educationally disadvantaged underclass, but it may be several more years before that recognition is translated into measurable dollars.

## Federated Campaigns

Corporate contributions to federated campaigns have historically represented the largest single expenditure in a company's charitable giving budget, and United Way contributions have represented the lion's share of federated human services campaigns, from 98% to 99 percent. Federated giving also accounts for the highest median dollar value of any single subcategory—$242,000 in 1986, compared to $235,000 in 1985. (See Table 13 on page 33 for a comparison of median federated giving by size of total contributions program.)

As noted earlier, corporate contributions to federated campaigns as a share of total contributions declined between 1985 and 1986. Among matched-case companies, total *dollars* to federated campaigns was down by almost 1%. All of the drop occurred in non-United Way giving, which fell from $4.6 million to $2.2 million; corporate contributions to United Way by the core companies rose from $206 to $207 million. In 1986, 48% of all health and human services giving reported to The Conference Board went to federated campaigns, down from 50% in 1985 and 56% in 1977.

Pronounced industry differences occur in the subcategory of federated giving (see Chart 17). Overall, companies in the service sector gave 19% of their total contributions through federated giving in 1986. Companies in the utilities, retail and wholesale trade, and banking industries—those with high visibility and significant markets in their local communities—placed an even higher priority (over 20%) on federated campaigns. In contrast, manufacturing companies limited this subcategory to 11% of total giving in 1986. Major exceptions in 1986 were older, heavy manufacturing industries with longstanding ties to federated campaigns, such as primary metals, paper, nonelectrical machinery, and fabricated metals industries. Food, beverage, and tobacco com-

---

### The Top Five Industry Leaders in Giving to Health and Human Services

*Aggregate Percent of Total Contributions*

| | |
|---|---|
| Utilities | 43% |
| Fabricated metals | 39 |
| Banking | 37 |
| Nonelectrical machinery | 37 |
| Retail and wholesale trade | 37 |

*Median Percent of Total Contributions*

| | |
|---|---|
| Primary metals | 51% |
| Stone, clay, and glass | 50 |
| Utilities | 46 |
| Banking | 45 |
| Transportation | 45 |

*Aggregate Dollar Value of Contributions ($ Millions)*

| | |
|---|---|
| Food, beverage, and tobacco | $70 |
| Electrical machinery | $66 |
| Petroleum and gas | $47 |
| Chemicals | $41 |
| Banking | $39 |

*Median Dollar Value of Contributions ($ Thousands)*

| | |
|---|---|
| Transportation equipment | $1,858 |
| Petroleum and gas | $1,410 |
| Pharmaceuticals | $1,051 |
| Telecommunications | $ 896 |
| Food, beverage, and tobacco | $ 843 |

---

panies gave the lowest proportion of total contributions to federated campaigns, 5 percent.

In 1986, dollars per employee to federated campaigns increased modestly from a median of $29 to $30, an increase more likely the result of fewer employees than of more dollars. Chart 18 (page 26) indicates the broad range of spending among different industries.

## Education

Corporate giving to education surged in 1986. Total dollars among matched-case companies increased by 17%, from $569 million to $665 million. When adjusted for the effect of a $40-million gift of property, giving to this category still rose by close to 10 percent. The median percent change among the core companies was also strong—over 12%—indicating that increases were widespread. The change was the highest median growth rate among the five major categories of beneficiaries.

The median for giving to education as a percent of total contributions also moved upward to 31% for all companies after three consecutive years at 29 percent. Manufacturing companies have historically given a greater proportion of their contributions to education than have service companies (see Chart 23 on page 30), and 1986 was consistent with that trend.

Chart 17:
### Contributions to Federated Campaigns as a Percentage of Total Giving to Health and Human Services, by Industry

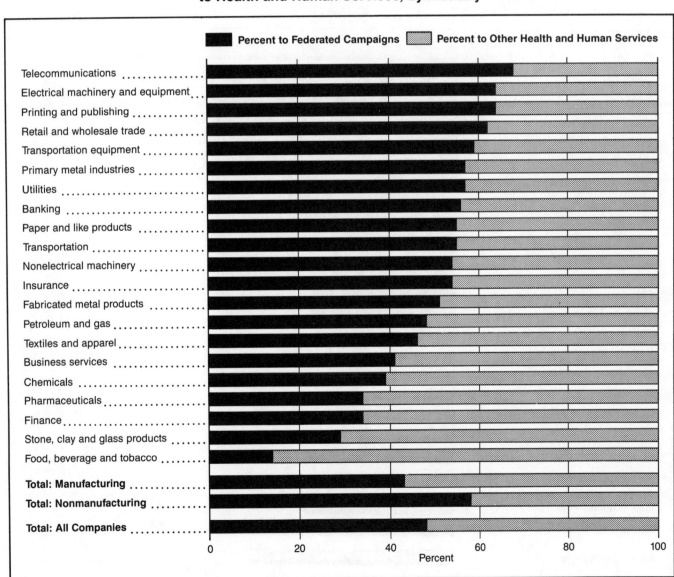

Manufacturers gave a median of 37% of their total giving, compared to a median of 26% for nonmanufacturers (see Appendix Table 17 on pages 52-53 for a summary of quartiles by industry). The median dollar values of giving to education also reflect the different priorities between the two industry sectors: Manufacturing companies gave a median of $651,000 to education while service companies contributed a median of $245,000.

### Higher Education

Corporate giving to educational organizations is essentially giving to *higher* education and, in recent years, this trend has intensified. In 1986, after adjusting for an extraordinary gift of property, nearly 28% of total contributions among survey respondents went to colleges and universities, up from less than 25% in 1976. As a percentage of total educational giving, higher education garnered 68% in 1986 compared to 66% in 1976. Total dollars to higher education more than tripled between 1976 and 1986.

In 1986, corporate giving to higher education occurred in five major areas: (1) departmental grants (7% of total contributions); (2) matching gifts (6%); (3) capital grants (5 %); (4) special project or research grants (5%); and (5) unrestricted institutional operating grants (4%).

Departmental, project and research grants came primarily from companies in the electrical machinery and equipment, telecommunications, and chemical industries, while the transportation equipment industry was the leader in unrestricted

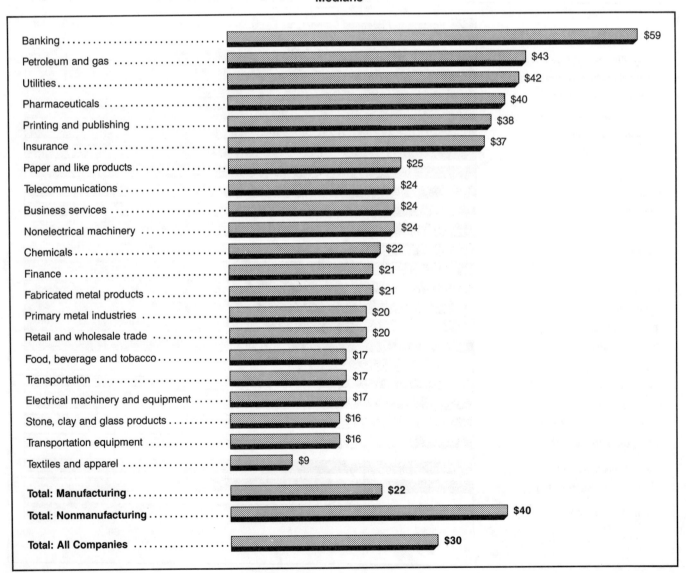

Chart 18:
## Contributions per Employee to Federated Campaigns, 1986
### Medians

| | |
|---|---|
| Banking | $59 |
| Petroleum and gas | $43 |
| Utilities | $42 |
| Pharmaceuticals | $40 |
| Printing and publishing | $38 |
| Insurance | $37 |
| Paper and like products | $25 |
| Telecommunications | $24 |
| Business services | $24 |
| Nonelectrical machinery | $24 |
| Chemicals | $22 |
| Finance | $21 |
| Fabricated metal products | $21 |
| Primary metal industries | $20 |
| Retail and wholesale trade | $20 |
| Food, beverage and tobacco | $17 |
| Transportation | $17 |
| Electrical machinery and equipment | $17 |
| Stone, clay and glass products | $16 |
| Transportation equipment | $16 |
| Textiles and apparel | $9 |
| **Total: Manufacturing** | $22 |
| **Total: Nonmanufacturing** | $40 |
| **Total: All Companies** | $30 |

operating grants. Capital grants more than doubled between 1984 and 1986 because of a $40 million gift of property. In general, corporate gifts to capital campaigns have been on the wane, declining from nearly 6% of total contributions in 1976 to approximately 2% in 1984. In 1986, however, even without the $40 million property donation, capital donations increased to nearly 3% of total contributions.

Matching gifts play a significant role in corporate contributions to higher education. Since 1976, matching gifts to colleges and universities have grown from $17 million to $99 million and from 3% to nearly 6% of total contributions. Several industries reported large shares in this subcategory: business services (14%); petroleum and gas (11%); and primary metals (10%). The median level for matching-gift programs to higher education was $121,000—the second-highest subcategory after United Way.

### Precollege Education

Although corporate involvement in *precollege* education has traditionally been minor, it appears to be slowly gaining ground. Total dollars to precollege beneficiaries increased from $6 million to $40 million between 1976 and 1986, and grew from 3% to over 5% as a percentage of total educational giving.

In 1986, approximately 43% of corporate support of precollege education—a total of $17 million—went to public schools. Another 22% took the form of employee matching gifts; the remaining 35% went to other precollege institutions. The median level of giving to public schools doubled from $5,000 to over $10,000 between 1984 and 1986. Petroleum and gas, paper, and financial services companies led in percentage of total contributions to public schools.

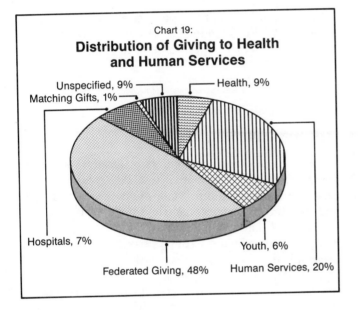

Chart 19:
**Distribution of Giving to Health and Human Services**

Unspecified, 9% — Health, 9%
Matching Gifts, 1%
Hospitals, 7%
Federated Giving, 48%
Human Services, 20%
Youth, 6%

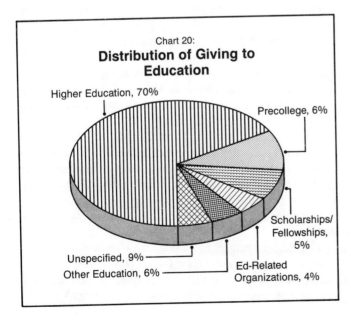

Chart 20:
**Distribution of Giving to Education**

Higher Education, 70%
Precollege, 6%
Scholarships/Fellowships, 5%
Ed-Related Organizations, 4%
Other Education, 6%
Unspecified, 9%

**The Top Five Industry Leaders in Giving to Education**

*Aggregate Percent of Total Contributions*

| | |
|---|---|
| Electrical machinery and equipment | 60% |
| Textiles and apparel | 57 |
| Printing and publishing | 52 |
| Petroleum and gas | 49 |
| Transportation equipment | 47 |

*Median Percent of Total Contributions*

| | |
|---|---|
| Petroleum and gas | 50% |
| Textiles and apparel | 47 |
| Electrical machinery and equipment | 43 |
| Chemicals | 39 |
| Pharmaceuticals | 38 |

*Aggregate Dollar Value of Contributions ($ Millions)*

| | |
|---|---|
| Electrical machinery | $179 |
| Petroleum and gas | $113 |
| Food, beverage, and tobacco | $ 81 |
| Chemicals | $ 66 |
| Transportation equipment | $ 63 |

*Median Dollar Value of Contributions ($ Thousands)*

| | |
|---|---|
| Transportation equipment | $3,840 |
| Petroleum and gas | $2,453 |
| Pharmaceuticals | $2,365 |
| Telecommunications | $2,350 |
| Electrical machinery | $1,360 |

## Culture and the Arts

Since 1980, survey participants have reported giving at least 11% of total contributions to cultural and arts organizations. In 1986, corporate contributions to the arts by survey companies approached $200 million and accounted for nearly 12% of all giving—its highest share since 1981. Growth was apparent in all measures: Contributions by the core group of companies rose by more than 10%, with a median change of 9 percent. The median gift to the arts was $135,000, up from $120,000 in 1985.

Shares of contributions to each of the subcategories of culture and the arts have remained comparatively stable over the last ten years. The leading beneficiary has consistently been museums, which received 2% of total contributions and 19% of all giving to the arts in 1986. Several industries report museums as a major priority: stone, clay and glass firms gave 32% of their total contributions; transportation companies gave 12%; and four other industries gave 4%—fabricated metals, paper, printing and publishing, and transportation equipment. The median dollar amount contributed to museums was $29,000.

Music has been another consistently funded subcategory, receiving about 1.5% of total contributions since 1977. In 1986, music was a priority among firms in retail and wholesale trade (4% of total contributions) and transportation companies (3%). Survey participants donated about $22 million to public television and radio as charitable contributions and another $552,000 as corporate assistance expenditures. Petroleum and gas companies and electrical equipment and machinery manufacturers led all other industries with donations of approximately $6 million each.

Since 1982, matching gifts to culture and the arts have represented about 1% of total contributions. Printing and publishing companies report that 2.5% of their charitable contributions in 1986—15% of their arts giving—was in the form of matching gifts. About one-third of the companies participating in the survey indicated that they made matching gifts in the arts, with a median of $37,000—the highest subcategory in culture and the arts.

The one subcategory to lose ground among culture and arts beneficiaries was cultural centers, which received .7% of total giving—their lowest share since 1975.

## The Top Five Industry Leaders in Giving to Culture and The Arts

*Aggregate Percent of Total Contributions*

| | |
|---|---:|
| Stone, clay and glass | 38% |
| Transportation | 21 |
| Fabricated metals | 21 |
| Retail and wholesale trade | 20 |
| Printing and publishing | 18 |

*Median Percent of Total Contributions*

| | |
|---|---:|
| Transportation | 19% |
| Printing and publishing | 19 |
| Telecommunications | 17 |
| Finance | 16 |
| Banking | 14 |

*Aggregate Dollar Value of Contributions ($ Millions)*

| | |
|---|---:|
| Petroleum and gas | $31 |
| Electrical machinery | $27 |
| Food, beverage, and tobacco | $20 |
| Telecommunications | $20 |
| Banking | $18 |

*Median Dollar Value of Contributions ($ Thousands)*

| | |
|---|---:|
| Telecommunications | $1,434 |
| Transportation equipment | $ 868 |
| Business services | $ 742 |
| Printing and publishing | $ 482 |
| Petroleum and gas | $ 411 |

## Civic and Community Activities

Giving to civic and community organizations and programs was down in 1986, both in total dollars and as a percent of total contributions. Among both the entire sample and the core companies, contributions in this category dropped 21%, and slid from 17% to 13% of total giving. As explained earlier, large gifts of property in recent years have been the underlying cause of the growth and subsequent contraction of giving in this category. Medians did show growth, however, indicating that, in general, companies are not abandoning civic and community beneficiaries.

In 1986, the median dollar value of contributions to civic and community organizations and programs was $149,000, an 18% increase over the 1985 median; and the median percent of total contributions was 11.9%, up from 11.5% in 1985. The median percent among service companies, in particular, climbed from 12.7% to 14.3% of total contributions. Among the core companies, the median change in giving for this category was a hike of nearly 7%.

Between 1984 and 1986, the balance of giving to civic and community activities shifted from national to local organizations, primarily because of the absence of large property gifts to national environmental groups in 1986. By 1986, two-thirds of the contributions to civic and community activities went to locally based groups, compared to two-fifths in 1984.

The major recipients of corporate donations in this category are programs that focus on community improvement, housing, and economic development, ranging from the national level, to that of the state, city, and neighborhood.

In 1986, a full 37% of giving to all civic and community groups (nearly 5% of total contributions) went to such organizations, up from 28% in 1984. In the late seventies and early eighties, however, the share was greater—between 41 and 47% of all civic and community contributions went to community improvement.

A number of major changes occurred between 1984 and 1986 in individual community improvement subcategories. Contributions to national groups plummeted from $30 million and over 2% of total contributions to $13 million and less than 1 percent. Corporate support of housing programs fell from $14 million and 1% of total giving, to $8 million and .5 percent. Aid to municipal and statewide groups, however, more than doubled, from $8 million and .5%, to $17 million and over 1% of total contributions. Grants for economic development and employment programs jumped from $10 million to $24.5 million.

The median contributions in these subcategories included $19,000 to neighborhood-based groups, $15,000 to national groups, $14,000 to economic development programs and $12,000 to housing programs. Industries with major participation in economic development programs include transportation equipment (7% of total contributions) and transportation (5%). Neighborhood groups received nearly 5% of fabricated metals' total contributions and nearly 4% from paper companies. Food, beverage, and tobacco companies gave over 4% of their total contributions to municipal and statewide groups. Primary metals, banking, and petroleum gave over 1% of total giving to housing.

Environmental and ecology groups received the next largest share of corporate donations for civic and community activities—16% of the category total and about 2% of total contributions. Zoos, parks, wildlife, and conservation organizations have been the major recipients of large parcels of land since 1983. However, total contributions to both national and local environmental groups are now down, from $97 million in 1984 to $36 million in 1986. The median gifts were $7,000 to national organizations and $10,000 to local

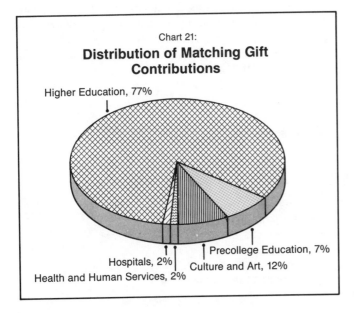

Chart 21:
**Distribution of Matching Gift Contributions**

Higher Education, 77%
Precollege Education, 7%
Culture and Art, 12%
Hospitals, 2%
Health and Human Services, 2%

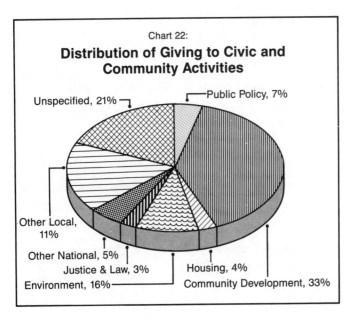

Chart 22:
**Distribution of Giving to Civic and Community Activities**

Unspecified, 21%
Public Policy, 7%
Other Local, 11%
Other National, 5%
Justice & Law, 3%
Environment, 16%
Housing, 4%
Community Development, 33%

**The Top Five Industry Leaders in Giving To Civic and Community Activities**

*Aggregate Percent of Total Contributions*

| | |
|---|---|
| Insurance | 28% |
| Retail and wholesale trade | 21 |
| Finance | 19 |
| Transportation | 18 |
| Utilities | 18 |

*Median Percent of Total Contributions*

| | |
|---|---|
| Transportation | 18% |
| Telecommunications | 17 |
| Banking | 16 |
| Retail and wholesale trade | 15 |
| Utilities | 15 |

*Aggregate Dollar Value of Contributions ($ Millions)*

| | |
|---|---|
| Petroleum and gas | $35 |
| Insurance | $29 |
| Chemicals | $22 |
| Food, beverage, and tobacco | $22 |
| Transportation equipment | $20 |

*Median Dollar Value ($ Thousands)*

| | |
|---|---|
| Telecommunications | $951 |
| Pharmaceuticals | $773 |
| Transportation equipment | $733 |
| Petroleum and gas | $499 |
| Food, beverage, and tobacco | $310 |

groups in 1986. Chemical companies, at 3% of their total contributions, and paper companies (2%), were the major funders of national environmental and ecology groups. Insurance companies gave 17% of their total contributions to local environmental groups.

Corporate contributions to public policy organizations have remained at approximately the same level since 1980 —at $15 to $16 million and 1% of total contributions. Pharmaceutical companies (3% of total contributions) and financial services firms (2%) were the leading industries in terms of the share of their total contributions.

Donations to other local organizations—groups that tackle transportation, fire and police protection, and housing issues at the local level—fell between 1985 and 1986, from 2.5% to 1.5% of total contributions. Transportation companies nevertheless gave 8% and utilities 7% of their total contributions to these causes.

## "Other" Organizations

Corporate contributions to "other" causes amounted to $68 million and represented just 4% of total giving in 1986—the lowest share since 1970. Total donations among the matched sample dropped 9% between 1985 and 1986, with a *median* change of -47 percent. The median level of giving for all companies in the 1986 survey was $33,000, a decrease of 28% from the 1985 median.

Nearly half of the giving in this category goes to U.S. groups that provide aid to other countries, which accounted for about 2% of total contributions in the 1986 Annual Survey. Historically, pharmaceutical companies have allocated a substantial portion of their contributions to this subcategory (particularly in the form of company product). In 1986, pharmaceutical companies gave 9%, down from 13% in 1984. In recent years, chemical companies have also donated sizable shares to aid to other countries—8% in 1986. In 1986, the median dollar value of gifts in this subcategory was $31,000, up from $19,000 in 1984.

Miscellaneous special events and programs received just over 1% of all contributions, with a median of $19,000. Several industries gave over 2% of their total contributions to this subcategory, including chemicals, pharmaceuticals, printing and publishing, finance, and retail and wholesale trade.

Religious organizations were the recipients of less than .1% of all corporate donations. Dollars to this subcategory have sharply declined in the last ten years; the $600,000 reported in 1986 was one-third of the amount donated in 1977. Only the textiles and apparel industry reported contributions amounting to 1% of their total giving.

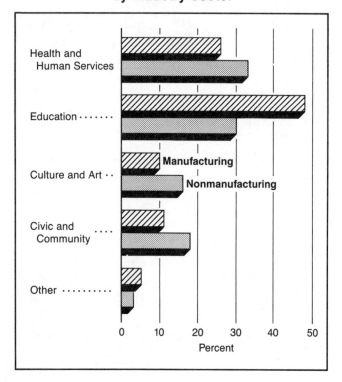

Chart 23:
**Distribution of Corporate Contributions by Industry Sector**

**The Top Five Industry Leaders in Giving to Other Groups**

*Aggregate Percent of Total Contributions*

| | |
|---|---|
| Pharmaceuticals | 12% |
| Chemicals | 11 |
| Finance | 5 |
| Banking | 4 |
| Transportation equipment | 4 |

*Median Percent of Total Contributions*

| | |
|---|---|
| Pharmaceuticals | 7% |
| Machinery, nonelectrical | 5 |
| Food, beverage, and tobacco | 4 |
| Finance | 4 |
| Transportation equipment | 4 |

*Aggregate Dollar Value of Contributions ($ Millions)*

| | |
|---|---|
| Chemicals | $17 |
| Electrical machinery | $13 |
| Pharmaceuticals | $ 9 |
| Food, beverage, and tobacco | $ 6 |
| Transportation equipment | $ 5 |

*Median Dollar Value of Contributions ($ Thousands)*

| | |
|---|---|
| Pharmaceuticals | $186 |
| Electrical machinery | $124 |
| Finance | $103 |
| Telecommunications | $ 98 |
| Transportation equipment | $ 97 |

## Regional Giving

For the third consecutive year, The Conference Board has analyzed the regional differences in corporate contributions, based on the *headquarters* location of the survey companies. The regional data presented in Table 14 on page 34 are based on the consolidated figures supplied to the Board by company representatives—usually headquarters based—who report the company's nationwide total.

The major differences highlighted by the regional data follow:

• According to survey results for 1986, companies headquartered in the Mid-Atlantic region (New York and New Jersey) lead the nation with the highest median total contributions—$3.8 million compared to $1.4 million nationally. The 61 companies reporting from this region gave a total of $518 million—nearly one-third of all contributions reported in the Annual Survey for 1986. Of the 75 largest donors in 1986, 21 are headquartered in the Mid-Atlantic region.

• The Pacific region was the headquarters of those companies with the highest median ratio of contributions to U.S. pretax income. The median of 2.1% was considerably higher than the national median of 1.17%. This is the first time that companies headquartered in the Breadbasket states did not lead in the contributions ratio.

• Three regions gave exceptionally high shares of their total contributions to education, in a year when education donations on the whole were up. In two of the regions, the proportions going to education represented significant shifts from past practice. Companies from the Southeast gave 53%—11% more than in 1985. In this region, the change was entirely the result of one $40-million gift of property. The median dollar value of giving to education in the Southeast was $295,000, one of the lowest in the country.

Firms headquartered in the Pacific region donated 49% of their total contributions to education, an increase of 8% over 1985. These increases may be attributable to the first-time participation of some new high-technology companies, which emphasize giving to education. The stress on giving to education in the Pacific region was also reflected by the median dollar value of gifts to education, which was $608,000—one of the highest in the country.

The third region to report a high level of educational contributions is New England, which has traditionally led in share of total giving devoted to education. In 1985 and 1986, companies headquartered in New England donated 47% of their total contributions to educational institutions.

• Companies from the Mountain states have always led in the proportion of giving to health and human services and continued to do so in 1986, with 50% of their total contributions in this category.

• Giving to the arts has consistently been a high priority for companies headquartered in the Breadbasket states (particularly Minnesota). In 1986, a total of 20% of survey companies' contributions went to culture and arts organizations, an increase of 3% over 1985. The median dollar value of giving to the arts by this region was $312,000 in 1986, the second-highest in the nation.

• In both 1985 and 1986, companies headquartered in the industrial states—mainly heavy manufacturers and basic metals companies in older urban communities—donated a sizable proportion of their contributions to civic and community activities.

# Table 12: Beneficiaries of Support Among 75 Largest Donors, 1986

| Company Rank | Contributions (Dollars) | Health and Human Services | Education | Culture and Arts | Civic and Community | Other |
|---|---|---|---|---|---|---|
| 1 | $111,900,000 | 22% | 63% | 9% | 3% | 3% |
| 2 | 72,076,000 | 25 | 68 | 3 | 3 | 1 |
| 3 | 56,115,192 | 19 | 63 | 3 | 9 | 6 |
| 4 | 46,563,622 | 20 | 58 | 12 | 7 | 0 |
| 5 | 46,099,967 | 12 | 52 | 22 | 14 | 1 |
| 6 | 34,973,597 | 22 | 48 | 14 | 13 | 3 |
| 7 | 32,949,125 | 11 | 87 | 1 | * | 1 |
| 8 | 30,900,000 | 15 | 58 | 4 | 18 | 5 |
| 9 | 29,747,359 | 15 | 15 | 2 | 66 | 3 |
| 10 | 26,141,026 | 25 | 45 | 12 | 18 | 0 |
| 11 | 25,830,431 | 12 | 48 | 12 | 29 | 0 |
| 12 | 24,940,506 | 23 | 36 | 29 | 7 | 5 |
| 13 | 23,886,000 | 33 | 39 | 8 | 6 | 13 |
| 14 | 21,700,000 | 22 | 67 | 5 | 4 | 3 |
| 15 | 21,306,000 | 45 | 42 | 2 | 10 | 0 |
| 16 | 20,781,538 | 25 | 11 | 44 | 21 | * |
| 17 | 19,750,222 | 37 | 25 | 9 | 29 | 0 |
| 18 | 19,154,503 | 20 | 63 | 7 | 9 | 1 |
| 19 | 17,883,448 | 13 | 43 | 14 | 15 | 15 |
| 20 | 17,654,000 | 24 | 54 | 9 | 12 | 1 |
| 21 | 17,566,562 | 27 | 45 | 14 | 10 | 3 |
| 22 | 17,263,356 | 82 | 5 | 9 | 4 | 0 |
| 23 | 15,146,933 | 6 | 17 | 1 | 1 | 75 |
| 24 | 14,750,000 | 36 | 41 | 17 | 5 | 0 |
| 25 | 14,631,404 | 27 | 34 | 17 | 16 | 6 |
| 26 | 14,297,171 | 27 | 49 | 11 | 9 | 3 |
| 27 | 13,290,510 | 27 | 35 | 22 | 8 | 8 |
| 28 | 13,006,438 | 22 | 52 | 11 | 15 | 1 |
| 29 | 12,868,199 | 14 | 12 | 3 | 71 | 1 |
| 30 | 12,377,815 | 43 | 23 | 23 | 10 | 1 |
| 31 | 12,337,985 | 34 | 43 | 14 | 9 | 0 |
| 32 | 12,000,000 | 40 | 26 | 23 | 11 | 0 |
| 33 | 11,952,682 | 27 | 4 | 1 | 69 | 0 |
| 34 | 11,647,000 | 56 | 16 | 6 | 15 | 7 |
| 35 | 10,768,448 | 13 | 48 | 4 | 31 | 5 |
| 36 | 10,746,200 | 43 | 30 | 11 | 16 | 0 |
| 37 | 10,487,160 | 25 | 48 | 13 | 12 | 2 |
| 38 | 10,480,308 | 25 | 31 | 6 | 35 | 3 |
| 39 | 10,478,548 | 24 | 37 | 28 | 11 | 1 |
| 40 | 10,427,982 | 44 | 26 | 17 | 12 | 2 |
| 41 | 10,352,585 | 26 | 26 | 24 | 19 | 6 |
| 42 | 10,259,781 | 23 | 29 | 37 | 10 | 1 |
| 43 | 10,051,138 | 28 | 32 | 29 | 7 | 4 |
| 44 | 9,803,589 | 34 | 39 | 11 | 12 | 4 |
| 45 | 9,642,457 | 28 | 30 | 19 | 17 | 6 |
| 46 | 9,583,000 | 40 | 41 | 9 | 10 | 0 |
| 47 | 9,466,526 | 3 | 88 | 5 | 2 | 1 |
| 48 | 9,438,352 | 26 | 33 | 24 | 16 | 2 |
| 49 | 9,381,957 | 26 | 33 | 17 | 24 | 1 |
| 50 | 8,874,672 | 4 | 95 | * | 1 | * |

Details in each row may not add to 100 percent due to rounding.

*Less than 1 percent.

## Table 12: Beneficiaries of Support Among 75 Largest Donors, 1986

| Company Rank | Contributions (Dollars) | Health and Human Services | Education | Culture and Arts | Civic and Community | Other |
|---|---|---|---|---|---|---|
| 51 | 8,697,524 | 47 | 23 | 11 | 19 | 0 |
| 52 | 8,570,204 | 39 | 40 | 21 | 0 | 0 |
| 53 | 8,425,955 | 26 | 38 | 15 | 14 | 7 |
| 54 | 8,306,909 | 35 | 28 | 17 | 20 | 0 |
| 55 | 8,262,778 | 53 | 24 | 10 | 12 | 1 |
| 56 | 8,107,494 | 35 | 50 | 8 | 6 | 1 |
| 57 | 7,935,225 | 32 | 20 | 4 | 18 | 26 |
| 58 | 7,867,459 | 28 | 42 | 12 | 18 | * |
| 59 | 7,695,000 | 32 | 32 | 13 | 23 | * |
| 60 | 7,687,473 | 4 | 84 | 1 | 1 | 11 |
| 61 | 7,659,849 | 31 | 40 | 10 | 20 | * |
| 62 | 7,568,820 | 74 | 18 | 5 | 2 | 1 |
| 63 | 7,533,880 | 40 | 32 | 8 | 18 | 2 |
| 64 | 7,461,431 | 20 | 60 | 12 | 5 | 4 |
| 65 | 7,386,522 | 8 | 64 | 5 | 17 | 6 |
| 66 | 7,363,023 | 39 | 16 | 15 | 18 | 13 |
| 67 | 7,278,297 | 28 | 31 | 14 | 15 | 12 |
| 68 | 7,163,541 | 10 | 88 | 2 | * | 0 |
| 69 | 6,971,414 | 29 | 35 | 16 | 19 | 0 |
| 70 | 6,945,000 | 21 | 52 | 3 | 6 | 18 |
| 71 | 6,615,481 | 34 | 30 | 14 | 17 | 5 |
| 72 | 6,599,806 | 15 | 44 | 20 | 21 | 0 |
| 73 | 6,531,007 | 31 | 45 | 14 | 8 | 2 |
| 74 | 6,267,193 | 4 | 38 | 24 | 31 | 3 |
| 75 | 6,003,720 | 36 | 57 | 5 | 2 | 0 |

*Less than 1 percent.
Total in a row may not add to 100 percent due to rounding.

## Table 13: Median Contribution to Federated Campaigns

| Program Size | Number of Companies | Median Contribution to Federated Campaign |
|---|---|---|
| Less than $500,000 . . . . . . . . | 83 | $   67,641 |
| $500,000 to $1 million . . . . . . . | 68 | 171,823 |
| $1 million to $5 million . . . . . . | 115 | 321,042 |
| $5 million and over . . . . . . . . | 80 | 1,412,785 |
| Total . . . . . . . . . . . . . . . . . . | 346 | $  242,487 |

## Table 14: Distribution of Corporate Contributions by Headquarters Region [a]

| Region | Number of Companies | Total Contributions ($ millions) | Federated Campaigns | Other Health and Human Services | Total Health and Human Services | Education | Culture and Arts | Civic and Community | Other |
|---|---|---|---|---|---|---|---|---|---|
| | | | | Health and Human Services | | | | | |
| New England ...................... (Maine, New Hampshire, Vermont, Massachusetts, Rhode Island, Connecticut) | 42 | $ 148.4 | 14% | 13% | 27% | 47% | 12% | 11% | 2% |
| Mid-Atlantic: ........................ (New York, New Jersey) | 61 | 517.8 | 12 | 12 | 24 | 44 | 15 | 13 | 4 |
| Industrial Heartland: ................. (Pennsylvania, Ohio, Michigan, Indiana, Illinois, Wisconsin) | 115 | 453.2 | 15 | 17 | 32 | 37 | 9 | 17 | 6 |
| Southeast: ......................... (Delaware, Maryland, Virginia, West Virginia, Kentucky, Tennessee, North Carolina, South Carolina, Georgia, Florida, Alabama, Mississippi) | 56 | 197.2 | 9 | 16 | 25 | 53 | 8 | 11 | 3 |
| Breadbasket: ....................... (Minnesota, Iowa, Missouri, Kansas, Nebraska, South Dakota, North Dakota) | 29 | 119.6 | 16 | 17 | 33 | 31 | 20 | 14 | 2 |
| Southwest: ......................... (Arkansas, Louisiana, Texas, Oklahoma) | 31 | 73.2 | 17 | 12 | 29 | 44 | 11 | 13 | 3 |
| Mountain States: ................... (Montana, Wyoming, Colorado, New Mexico, Arizona, Utah, Nevada, Idaho) | 4 | 2.3 | 20 | 30 | 50 | 22 | 13 | 9 | 6 |
| Pacific ............................ (Washington, Oregon, California, Alaska, Hawaii) | 32 | 162.3 | 16 | 14 | 30 | 49 | 9 | 9 | 3 |
| Total ......................... | 370 | $1,674.0 | 13% | 15% | 28% | 43% | 12% | 13% | 4% |

[a]Total for a region may not add to 100 percent because of rounding.

# Appendix Tables

## Table 1: Corporate Contributions and Corporate Income Before and After Taxes[1]

| Year | Amount ($ Millions) | Income[3] before Taxes ($ Millions) | Contributions As Percent of Income before Taxes | Income[3] after Taxes ($ Millions) | As Percent of Income after Taxes |
|---|---|---|---|---|---|
| 1936......................... | $ 30 | $ 7,900 | 0.38% | $ 4,900 | 0.61% |
| 1937......................... | 33 | 7,900 | 0.42 | 5,300 | 0.62 |
| 1938......................... | 27 | 4,100 | 0.65 | 2,900 | 0.93 |
| 1939......................... | 31 | 7,200 | 0.43 | 5,700 | 0.54 |
| 1940......................... | 38 | 10,000 | 0.38 | 7,200 | 0.53 |
| 1941......................... | 58 | 17,900 | 0.32 | 10,300 | 0.56 |
| 1942......................... | 98 | 21,700 | 0.45 | 10,300 | 0.95 |
| 1943......................... | 159 | 25,300 | 0.63 | 11,200 | 1.42 |
| 1944......................... | 234 | 24,200 | 0.97 | 11,300 | 2.07 |
| 1945......................... | 266 | 19,800 | 1.34 | 9,100 | 2.92 |
| 1946......................... | 214 | 24,800 | 0.86 | 15,700 | 1.36 |
| 1947......................... | 241 | 31,800 | 0.76 | 20,500 | 1.18 |
| 1948......................... | 239 | 35,600 | 0.67 | 23,200 | 1.03 |
| 1949......................... | 223 | 29,200 | 0.76 | 19,000 | 1.17 |
| 1950......................... | 252 | 42,900 | 0.59 | 25,000 | 1.01 |
| 1951......................... | 343 | 44,500 | 0.77 | 21,900 | 1.57 |
| 1952......................... | 399 | 39,600 | 1.01 | 20,200 | 1.98 |
| 1953......................... | 495 | 41,200 | 1.20 | 20,900 | 2.37 |
| 1954......................... | 314 | 38,700 | 0.81 | 21,100 | 1.49 |
| 1955......................... | 415 | 49,200 | 0.84 | 27,200 | 1.53 |
| 1956......................... | 418 | 49,600 | 0.84 | 27,600 | 1.51 |
| 1957......................... | 419 | 48,100 | 0.87 | 26,700 | 1.57 |
| 1958......................... | 395 | 41,900 | 0.94 | 22,900 | 1.72 |
| 1959......................... | 482 | 52,600 | 0.92 | 28,900 | 1.67 |
| 1960......................... | 482 | 49,800 | 0.97 | 27,100 | 1.78 |
| 1961......................... | 512 | 49,700 | 1.03 | 26,900 | 1.90 |
| 1962......................... | 595 | 55,000 | 1.08 | 31,100 | 1.91 |
| 1963......................... | 657 | 59,600 | 1.10 | 33,400 | 1.97 |
| 1964......................... | 729 | 66,500 | 1.10 | 38,500 | 1.89 |
| 1965......................... | 785 | 77,200 | 1.02 | 46,300 | 1.70 |
| 1966......................... | 805 | 83,000 | 0.97 | 49,400 | 1.63 |
| 1967......................... | 830 | 79,700 | 1.04 | 47,200 | 1.76 |
| 1968......................... | 1,005 | 88,500 | 1.13 | 49,400 | 2.03 |
| 1969......................... | 1,055 | 86,700 | 1.22 | 47,200 | 2.24 |
| 1970......................... | 797 | 75,400 | 1.06 | 41,300 | 1.93 |
| 1971......................... | 865 | 86,600 | 1.00 | 49,000 | 1.76 |
| 1972......................... | 1,009 | 100,600 | 1.00 | 58,900 | 1.71 |
| 1973......................... | 1,174 | 125,600 | 0.93 | 76,600 | 1.53 |
| 1974......................... | 1,200 | 136,700 | 0.88 | 85,100 | 1.41 |
| 1975......................... | 1,202 | 132,100 | 0.91 | 81,500 | 1.47 |
| 1976......................... | 1,487 | 166,300 | 0.89 | 102,500 | 1.45 |
| 1977......................... | 1,791 | 200,400 | 0.89 | 127,400 | 1.41 |
| 1978......................... | 2,084 | 233,500 | 0.89 | 150,000 | 1.39 |
| 1979......................... | 2,288 | 257,200 | 0.89 | 169,200 | 1.35 |
| 1980......................... | 2,359 | 237,100 | 0.99 | 152,300 | 1.55 |
| 1981......................... | 2,514 | 226,500 | 1.11 | 145,400 | 1.73 |
| 1982......................... | 2,906 | 169,600 | 1.71 | 106,500 | 2.73 |
| 1983......................... | 3,627 | 207,600 | 1.75 | 130,400 | 2.78 |
| 1984......................... | 4,057 | 240,000 | 1.69 | 146,100 | 2.78 |
| 1985......................... | 4,400(est.)[2] | 224,800 | 1.96 | 128,100 | 3.43 |
| 1986......................... | $4,500(est.)[2] | $231,900 | 1.94 | $126,800 | 3.55 |

[1]Reflects total consolidated corporate income before and after taxes.

[2]From Council for Aid to Education.

[3]The income figures on this table have been adjusted to coincide with recently updated data issued by the Department of Commerce. Thus, some of the figures in the income columns, and the ratios based upon them, will differ slightly from those published here previously.

Note: Figures in this table reflect contributions and income of *all* U.S. corporations. Figures in all other tables in this report are based solely on responses by survey participants.

*Sources:* Department of Commerce, Internal Revenue Service.

## Table 2: Contributions as a Percent of Pretax Income, Quartiles, 1977 to 1986[1]

| | Contributions as a Percent of U.S. Income | | | Contributions as a Percent of Worldwide Income | | |
|---|---|---|---|---|---|---|
| | Lower Quartile | Median | Upper Quartile | Lower Quartile | Median | Upper Quartile |
| 1977 | 0.36% | 0.67% | 1.00% | 0.35% | 0.61% | 1.05% |
| 1978 | 0.36 | 0.66 | 1.20 | 0.34 | 0.58 | 0.98 |
| 1979 | 0.40 | 0.69 | 1.15 | 0.36 | 0.50 | 1.00 |
| 1980 | 0.40 | 0.73 | 1.34 | 0.37 | 0.66 | 1.16 |
| 1981 | 0.40 | 0.81 | 1.47 | 0.40 | 0.72 | 1.23 |
| 1982 | 0.54 | 1.13 | 1.85 | 0.53 | 0.99 | 1.62 |
| 1983 | 0.63 | 1.12 | 1.97 | 0.52 | 0.94 | 1.65 |
| 1984 | 0.56 | 1.03 | 1.88 | 0.53 | 0.85 | 1.54 |
| 1985 | 0.63 | 1.18 | 2.04 | 0.58 | 0.99 | 1.60 |
| 1986 | 0.66 | 1.17 | 2.18 | 0.59 | 1.01 | 1.63 |

[1] In each table using medians or quartiles, the data for each group (e.g., an industry class, an asset or income-size group) are placed in rank order from the lowest to the highest value, and divided into quarters. The first quartile is 25 percent of the way from the bottom number in the ranking; the median is the middle value in the ranking; and the third quartile is then 75 percent of the way between the lowest and the highest value. The "total" line on each table provides the quartiles (or median) for all of the companies included in that table.

## Table 3: Structure of Corporate Contributions, 1982-1986
(millions of dollars)

| | 1986 | 1985 | 1984 | 1983 | 1982 |
|---|---|---|---|---|---|
| Total company contributions | $1,688.6 (353) | $1,666.5 (423) | $1,448.9 (404) | $1,250.7 (484) | $1,116.8 (519) |
| Less: Grants to company foundations | 649.1 (157) | 614.0 (182) | 562.2 (157) | 435.7 (159) | 367.1 (186) |
| Other company contributions | 1,039.5 (334) | 1,052.5 (395) | 886.7 (388) | 815.0 (461) | 749.7 (494) |
| Plus: Contributions by company foundations | 641.0 (224) | 658.4 (256) | 569.2 (230) | 553.0 (270) | 531.9 (286) |
| Total corporate contributions | $1,680.4 (372) | $1,710.9 (439) | $1,455.9 (422) | $1,368.0 (503) | $1,281.6 (534) |

(Numbers in parentheses are counts of non-zero answers).

## Table 4: Relationship of Foundation Payouts to Pay-ins, 1982-1986
(millions of dollars)

| Category | 1986 | 1985 | 1984 | 1983 | 1982 |
|---|---|---|---|---|---|
| Grants to company foundations | $649.1 | $614.0 | $562.2 | $435.7 | $367.1 |
| Contributions by company foundations | 641.0 | 658.4 | 569.2 | 553.0 | 531.9 |
| Payouts less pay-ins | (8.1) | 44.4 | 7.0 | 117.3 | 164.8 |
| Percent payouts exceeded (were less than) pay-ins | −1.25% | 7.23% | 1.25% | 26.92% | 44.89% |

**Table 5: Flow of Funds Into and Out of Company Foundations, 1982 to 1986**

| | 1986 | | 1985 | | 1984 | | 1983 | | 1982 | |
|---|---|---|---|---|---|---|---|---|---|---|
| | Number of Companies | Percent of Total | Number of Companies | Percent of Total | Number of Companies | Percent of Total | Number of Companies | Percent of Total | Number of Companies | Percent of Total |
| Pay-ins equal to payouts....... | 22 | 9% | 25 | 9% | 16 | 7% | 7 | 2% | 8 | 3% |
| Pay-ins less than payouts...... | 136 | 57 | 162 | 60 | 143 | 59 | 187 | 69 | 192 | 67 |
| Pay-ins greater than payouts ... | 82 | 34 | 82 | 30 | 84 | 34 | 78 | 29 | 86 | 30 |
| Total ..................... | 240 | 100% | 269 | 100% | 243 | 100% | 272 | 100% | 286 | 100% |

**Table 6: Contributions as a Percent of Pretax Income, 1986—**
Companies Grouped by Rate of Giving

| | U.S. Pretax Income | | | | | |
|---|---|---|---|---|---|---|
| Contributions as Percent of Pretax Income | All Companies | Manufacturing | Banking | Insurance[1] | Utilities and Telecommunication | Other Service |
| | (Number of Companies)[2] | | | | | |
| 0- .24% .............. | 25 | 3 | — | 2 | 19 | 1 |
| .25- .49 ................ | 30 | 9 | — | 4 | 16 | 1 |
| .50- .74 ................ | 28 | 16 | 3 | 1 | 5 | 3 |
| .75- .99 ................ | 37 | 17 | 9 | 7 | 2 | 2 |
| 1.0-1.49 ................ | 57 | 27 | 14 | 5 | 4 | 7 |
| 1.5-1.99 ................ | 30 | 16 | 8 | 5 | — | 1 |
| 2.0-2.99 ................ | 31 | 21 | 4 | 1 | 2 | 3 |
| 3.0-3.99 ................ | 17 | 11 | 2 | 2 | 2 | — |
| 4.0-4.99 ................ | 14 | 11 | — | 1 | — | 2 |
| 5.0 and over ............ | 18 | 15 | — | 2 | — | 1 |
| Total ................. | 287 | 146 | 40 | 30 | 50 | 21 |

| | Worldwide Pretax Income | | | | | |
|---|---|---|---|---|---|---|
| Contributions as Percent of Pretax Income | All Companies | Manufacturing | Banking | Insurance[1] | Utilities and Telecommunication | Other Service |
| | (Number of Companies)[3] | | | | | |
| 0- .24% .............. | 26 | 3 | — | 2 | 20 | 1 |
| .25- .49 ................ | 38 | 16 | — | 4 | 16 | 2 |
| .50- .74 ................ | 46 | 27 | 5 | 2 | 7 | 5 |
| .75- .99 ................ | 49 | 25 | 10 | 9 | 2 | 3 |
| 1.0-1.49 ................ | 68 | 35 | 15 | 5 | 4 | 9 |
| 1.5-1.99 ................ | 31 | 18 | 7 | 4 | 2 | — |
| 2.0-2.99 ................ | 22 | 16 | 3 | 1 | 1 | 1 |
| 3.0-3.99 ................ | 16 | 12 | 1 | 2 | 1 | — |
| 4.0-4.99 ................ | 10 | 4 | 1 | 2 | 1 | 2 |
| 5.0 and over ............ | 13 | 10 | — | 2 | — | 1 |
| Total ................. | 319 | 166 | 42 | 33 | 54 | 24 |

[1] Insurance company figures are based on "net gain from operations after dividends to policyholders and before federal income tax, excluding capital gains and losses"—the closest measure to pretax income of corporations generally.
[2] 38 loss companies excluded.
[3] 32 loss companies excluded.

**Table 7A: Contributions as a Percent of U.S. Pretax Income, 1986**
Companies Grouped by Industry Class[1]

| Industrial Classification | Number of Companies | U.S. Pretax Income (Sum) ($ Millions) | Contributions (Sum) ($ Thousands) | U.S. Pretax Income (Median) ($ Thousands) | Contributions (Median) ($ Thousands) | Contributions as a Percent of U.S. Pretax Income (Median) |
|---|---|---|---|---|---|---|
| Chemicals | 24 | $ 7,620 | $ 147,539 | $ 130,518 | $2,726 | 2.04% |
| Electrical machinery and equipment | 24 | 10,110 | 280,014 | 134,332 | 2,781 | 2.02 |
| Fabricated metal products | 5 | 365 | 4,541 | 73,460 | 718 | 1.06 |
| Food, beverage and tobacco | 20 | 8,609 | 194,099 | 242,220 | 4,252 | 1.78 |
| Machinery, nonelectrical | 9 | 896 | 16,083 | 77,674 | 866 | 1.29 |
| Paper and like products | 11 | 1,793 | 18,818 | 151,371 | 1,508 | 0.91 |
| Petroleum and gas[2] | 14 | 5,707 | 146,222 | 178,478 | 3,392 | 2.37 |
| Pharmaceuticals | 8 | 3,422 | 60,992 | 491,800 | 5,972 | 1.30 |
| Primary metal industries | 5 | 416 | 12,487 | 69,200 | 584 | 1.41 |
| Printing and publishing | 5 | 1,492 | 22,508 | 266,846 | 3,783 | 1.42 |
| Stone, clay and glass products | 6 | 868 | 8,484 | 109,066 | 454 | 0.76 |
| Textiles and apparel | 5 | 454 | 6,213 | 95,951 | 709 | 0.81 |
| Transportation equipment[3] | 10 | 6,705 | 123,626 | 219,300 | 7,481 | 1.69 |
| Total: Manufacturing | 146 | $ 48,457 | $1,041,626 | 153,126 | 2,241 | 1.51 |
| Banking | 40 | 6,459 | 91,650 | 81,385 | 1,087 | 1.33 |
| Business services[4] | 5 | 519 | 5,970 | 60,362 | 525 | 1.35 |
| Finance | 3 | 621 | 5,883 | * | * | * |
| Insurance[5] | 30 | 6,900 | 74,884 | 98,336 | 726 | 1.03 |
| Retail and wholesale trade | 11 | 4,554 | 61,953 | 159,342 | 1,739 | 1.03 |
| Telecommunications | 9 | 9,159 | 46,224 | 556,876 | 5,200 | 0.69 |
| Transportation | 2 | 122 | 2,565 | * | * | * |
| Utilities | 41 | 14,937 | 43,135 | 257,262 | 635 | 0.31 |
| Total: Nonmanufacturing | 141 | $ 43,271 | $ 332,264 | 137,435 | 958 | .90 |
| Total: All Companies | 287 | $ 91,728 | $1,373,890 | 147,000 | 1,402 | 1.17 |

[1]Loss companies excluded.

[2]Includes mining companies.

[3]Includes tire manufacturers.

[4]Includes engineering and construction companies.

[5]Insurance company figures are based on "net gain from operations after dividends to policyholders and before federal income tax, excluding capital gains and losses"—the closest measure to pretax income of corporations generally.

*Industries with fewer than 5 cases are excluded.

**Table 7B: Contributions as a Percent of Worldwide Pretax Income, 1986**
Companies Grouped by Industry Class[1]

| Industrial Classification | Number of Companies | Worldwide Pretax Income (Sum) ($ Millions) | Contributions (Sum) ($ Thousands) | Worldwide Pretax Income (Median) ($ Thousands) | Contributions (Median) ($ Thousands) | Percent of Contributions to Worldwide Pretax Income (Median) |
|---|---|---|---|---|---|---|
| Chemicals | 26 | $ 12,258 | $ 150,568 | $ 212,060 | $2,420 | 1.14% |
| Electrical machinery and equipment | 26 | 19,243 | 290,449 | 260,033 | 3,274 | 1.32 |
| Fabricated metal products | 5 | 515 | 4,541 | 110,300 | 718 | 0.89 |
| Food, beverage and tobacco | 22 | 12,103 | 196,390 | 357,497 | 3,362 | 1.50 |
| Machinery, nonelectrical | 13 | 1,104 | 20,774 | 42,032 | 866 | 2.43 |
| Paper and like products | 11 | 2,067 | 18,818 | 158,896 | 1,508 | 0.74 |
| Petroleum and gas[2] | 18 | 22,101 | 200,085 | 374,613 | 7,404 | 1.18 |
| Pharmaceuticals | 9 | 6,311 | 68,526 | 876,300 | 8,945 | 0.89 |
| Primary metal industries | 5 | 447 | 12,487 | 81,300 | 584 | 1.41 |
| Printing and publishing | 9 | 2,157 | 30,963 | 266,562 | 3,142 | 1.42 |
| Stone, clay and glass products | 6 | 984 | 8,484 | 125,116 | 454 | 0.68 |
| Textiles and apparel | 5 | 500 | 6,213 | 104,050 | 709 | 0.75 |
| Transportation equipment[3] | 11 | 11,285 | 134,105 | 257,300 | 10,479 | 1.61 |
| Total: Manufacturing | 166 | $ 91,075 | $1,142,403 | 214,013 | 2,400 | 1.19 |
| Banking | 42 | 9,130 | 98,396 | 96,492 | 1,087 | 1.14 |
| Business services[4] | 6 | 764 | 7,368 | 77,217 | 546 | 0.92 |
| Finance | 4 | 1,228 | 9,592 | * | * | * |
| Insurance[5] | 33 | 8,175 | 91,488 | 113,326 | 941 | 0.99 |
| Retail and wholesale trade | 12 | 4,875 | 62,974 | 160,252 | 1,721 | 1.02 |
| Telecommunications | 12 | 16,557 | 115,593 | 1,736,500 | 6,135 | 0.64 |
| Transportation | 2 | 135 | 2,565 | * | * | * |
| Utilities | 42 | 15,251 | 43,698 | 253,530 | 629 | 0.27 |
| Total: Nonmanufacturing | 153 | $ 56,115 | $ 431,674 | 159,342 | 1,021 | .88 |
| Total: All Companies | 319 | $147,190 | $1,574,077 | 175,000 | 1,508 | 1.01 |

[1]Loss companies excluded.

[2]Includes mining companies.

[3]Includes tire manufacturers.

[4]Includes engineering and construction companies.

[5]Insurance company figures are based on "net gain from operations after dividends to policyholders and before federal income tax, excluding capital gains and losses"—the closest measure to pretax income of corporations generally.

*Industries with fewer than 5 cases are excluded.

# Table 8A: Charitable Contributions of 75 Largest Donors as a Percent of U.S. and Worldwide Pretax Income, 1986

| Company Rank | Contributions[1] (dollars) | U.S. Pretax Income[2] ($ Thousands) | Contributions as Percent of U.S. Pretax Income | Worldwide Pretax Income[2] ($ Thousands) | Contributions as Percent of Worldwide Pretax Income |
|---|---|---|---|---|---|
| 1 | $111,900,000 | $ 2,500,000 | 4.44% | $ 8,400,000 | 1.33% |
| 2 | 72,076,000 | 1,300,000 | 5.46 | 1,900,000 | 1.76 |
| 3 | 56,110,101 | 900,000 | 6.30 | 2,700,000 | 2.04 |
| 4 | 46,563,622 | n.a. | n.a. | 2,300,000 | 2.01 |
| 5 | 46,099,967 | 2,200,000 | 2.14 | 8,500,000 | 0.55 |
| 6 | 34,973,597 | 3,100,000 | 1.14 | 3,700,000 | 0.95 |
| 7 | 32,949,125 | 300,000 | 10.80 | 800,000 | 4.22 |
| 8 | 30,900,000 | 1,600,000 | 1.99 | 3,000,000 | 1.04 |
| 9 | 29,747,359 | 300,000 | 10.09 | 300,000 | 8.65 |
| 10 | 26,141,026 | 1,000,000 | 2.60 | 1,300,000 | 2.01 |
| 11 | 25,830,431 | 700,000 | 3.79 | 1,600,000 | 1.63 |
| 12 | 24,940,506 | 2,400,000 | 1.04 | 2,800,000 | 0.89 |
| 13 | 23,886,000 | 500,000 | 4.95 | 1,100,000 | 2.23 |
| 14 | 21,700,000 | 300,000 | 8.54 | 700,000 | 3.21 |
| 15 | 21,306,000 | 1,000,000 | 2.28 | 1,200,000 | 1.81 |
| 16 | 20,781,538 | 500,000 | 4.21 | 500,000 | 4.21 |
| 17 | 19,750,222 | 1,700,000 | 1.16 | 1,800,000 | 1.08 |
| 18 | 19,154,503 | n.a. | n.a. | 1,400,000 | 1.41 |
| 19 | 17,883,448 | n.. | n.a. | 3,000,000 | 0.60 |
| 20 | 17,654,000 | 200,000 | 9.97 | 1,700,000 | 1.01 |
| 21 | 17,566,562 | 800,000 | 2.10 | 1,300,000 | 1.30 |
| 22 | 17,263,356 | 200,000 | 7.15 | 400,000 | 4.85 |
| 23 | 15,146,933 | 700,000 | 2.20 | 800,000 | 1.85 |
| 24 | 14,750,000 | 1,000,000 | 1.43 | 1,000,000 | 1.43 |
| 25 | 14,631,404 | 2,900,000 | 0.50 | 5,000,000 | 0.29 |
| 26 | 14,297,171 | 300,000 | 4.69 | 600,000 | 2.39 |
| 27 | 13,290,510 | 400,000 | 3.47 | 900,000 | 1.55 |
| 28 | 13,006,438 | * | * | * | * |
| 29 | 12,868,199 | 100,000 | 10.20 | 200,000 | 5.40 |
| 30 | 12,377,815 | n.a. | n.a. | 2,100,000 | 0.59 |
| 31 | 12,337,985 | 900,000 | 1.37 | 1,100,000 | 1.17 |
| 32 | 12,000,000 | 1,700,000 | 0.69 | 1,700,000 | 0.69 |
| 33 | 11,952,682 | 300,000 | 4.15 | 400,000 | 3.06 |
| 34 | 11,647,000 | 900,000 | 1.26 | 900,000 | 1.26 |
| 35 | 10,768,448 | 500,000 | 2.18 | 1,200,000 | 0.87 |
| 36 | 10,746,200 | 600,000 | 1.85 | 700,000 | 1.51 |
| 37 | 10,487,160 | 100,000 | 15.15 | 100,000 | 12.90 |
| 38 | 10,480,308 | 700,000 | 1.60 | 900,000 | 1.16 |
| 39 | 10,478,548 | * | * | 100,000 | 8.46 |
| 40 | 10,427,982 | n.a. | n.a. | 2,900,000 | 0.36 |
| 41 | 10,352,585 | 800,000 | 1.36 | 1,700,000 | 0.61 |
| 42 | 10,259,781 | n.a. | n.a. | 200,000 | 4.35 |
| 43 | 10,051,138 | 400,000 | 2.59 | 700,000 | 1.48 |
| 44 | 9,803,589 | 500,000 | 2.12 | 600,000 | 1.54 |
| 45 | 9,642,457 | 700,000 | 1.47 | 800,000 | 1.14 |
| 46 | 9,583,000 | 800,000 | 1.22 | 800,000 | 1.20 |
| 47 | 9,466,526 | 300,000 | 3.34 | 300,000 | 3.20 |
| 48 | 9,438,352 | n.a. | n.a. | 1,800,000 | 0.52 |
| 49 | 9,381,957 | 1,200,000 | 0.79 | 1,200,000 | 0.78 |
| 50 | 8,874,673 | 100,000 | 9.34 | 100,000 | 7.55 |

[1]Direct giving and company foundation pay-outs included; grants made to and retained by company foundations are excluded.

[2]Domestic and worldwide pretax income rounded, percentages actual.

*Company showed loss.

n.a. = Not available.

# Table 8A: Charitable Contributions of 75 Largest Donors as a Percent of U.S. and Worldwide Pretax Income, 1985 (continued)

| Company Rank | Contributions[1] (dollars) | U.S. Pretax Income[2] ($ Thousands) | Contributions as Percent of U.S. Pretax Income | Worldwide Pretax Income[2] ($ Thousands) | Contributions as Percent of Worldwide Pretax Income |
|---|---|---|---|---|---|
| 51 | 8,697,524 | 300,000 | 2.85 | 300,000 | 2.69 |
| 52 | 8,570,204 | n.a. | n.a. | * | * |
| 53 | 8,425,955 | 400,000 | 2.32 | 500,000 | 1.72 |
| 54 | 8,306,909 | 2,000,000 | 0.42 | 2,000,000 | 0.42 |
| 55 | 8,262,778 | 700,000 | 1.16 | 900,000 | 0.89 |
| 56 | 8,107,494 | * | * | * | * |
| 57 | 7,935,225 | 600,000 | 1.24 | 900,000 | 0.91 |
| 58 | 7,867,459 | * | * | * | * |
| 59 | 7,695,000 | 500,000 | 1.52 | 600,000 | 1.30 |
| 60 | 7,687,473 | n.a. | n.a. | n.a. | n.a. |
| 61 | 7,659,849 | 200,000 | 3.77 | 200,000 | 3.27 |
| 62 | 7,568,820 | 200,000 | 3.20 | 300,000 | 2.40 |
| 63 | 7,533,880 | n.a. | n.a. | 1,000,000 | 0.78 |
| 64 | 7,461,431 | 400,000 | 1.87 | 500,000 | 1.61 |
| 65 | 7,386,522 | * | * | 700,000 | 1.07 |
| 66 | 7,363,023 | 200,000 | 3.63 | 200,000 | 4.15 |
| 67 | 7,278,297 | 400,000 | 1.98 | 1,200,000 | 0.62 |
| 68 | 7,163,541 | * | * | 40,000 | 16.92 |
| 69 | 6,971,414 | 700,000 | 1.04 | 700,000 | 0.99 |
| 70 | 6,945,000 | 700,000 | 1.06 | 1,100,000 | 0.65 |
| 71 | 6,615,481 | 300,000 | 1.89 | 400,000 | 1.75 |
| 72 | 6,599,806 | 700,000 | 0.95 | 1,500,000 | 0.44 |
| 73 | 6,531,007 | 200,000 | 2.73 | 400,000 | 1.77 |
| 74 | 6,267,193 | 200,000 | 3.51 | 200,000 | 3.51 |
| 75 | 6,003,720 | 600,000 | 1.08 | 600,000 | 1.08 |

[1]Direct giving and company foundation pay-outs included; grants made to and retained by company foundations are excluded.

[2]Domestic and worldwide pretax income rounded, percentages actual.

*Company showed loss.

n.a. = Not available.

# Table 8B: Corporate Social Expenditures of 75 Largest Donors as a Percent of U.S. and Worldwide Pretax Income

| Company Rank | Total Corporate Social Expenditure | Corporate Social Expenditure As A Percent of | | Rank for Corporate Assistance Only |
|---|---|---|---|---|
| | | U.S. Pretax Income | Worldwide Pretax Income | |
| 1 | $136,000,000 | 5.40 | 1.03 | I |
| 2 | 75,804,000 | 5.74 | 3.95 | 17 |
| 3 | 47,500,000 | 3.05 | 1.59 | 3 |
| 4 | 46,563,622 | n.a. | 2.01 | 155 |
| 5 | 43,615,533 | 4.66 | 3.71 | 2 |
| 6 | 41,804,978 | 1.36 | 1.13 | 8 |
| 7 | 38,171,000 | 15.03 | 5.65 | 4 |
| 8 | 35,909,410 | 1.50 | 1.28 | 6 |
| 9 | 33,014,759 | 11.20 | 9.60 | 20 |
| 10 | 30,266,734 | 3.01 | 2.32 | 15 |
| 11 | 28,247,431 | 4.15 | 1.78 | 25 |
| 12 | 25,109,000 | 5.20 | 2.34 | 39 |
| 13 | 22,162,915 | 4.48 | n.a. | 33 |
| 14 | 19,557,507 | 2.33 | 1.45 | 27 |
| 15 | 19,183,448 | * | 0.64 | 34 |
| 16 | 18,339,000 | 2.33 | 2.29 | 7 |
| 17 | 17,494,965 | 7.25 | 4.92 | 76 |
| 18 | 17,352,171 | 5.69 | 2.90 | 21 |
| 19 | 16,107,947 | 319.22 | 6.63 | 5 |
| 20 | 14,756,403 | n.a. | 6.25 | 12 |
| 21 | 14,720,000 | 1.43 | 1.43 | 153 |
| 22 | 13,569,589 | 2.94 | 2.13 | 16 |
| 23 | 13,526,419 | n.a. | 0.64 | 41 |
| 24 | 12,781,842 | n.a. | * | 14 |
| 25 | 12,317,000 | 1.33 | 1.33 | 50 |
| 26 | 12,302,585 | 1.61 | 0.72 | 28 |
| 27 | 12,228,861 | 1.86 | 1.45 | 24 |
| 28 | 11,891,707 | 17.18 | 14.63 | 32 |
| 29 | 11,384,549 | 0.96 | 0.94 | 26 |
| 30 | 10,663,248 | 0.53 | 0.53 | 10 |
| 31 | 10,304,502 | 2.95 | 2.73 | 18 |
| 32 | 10,143,064 | 2.80 | 2.07 | 30 |
| 33 | 10,042,658 | 3.06 | 2.81 | 13 |
| 34 | 9,937,310 | n.a. | n.a. | 22 |
| 35 | 9,747,318 | 3.44 | 3.30 | 73 |
| 36 | 9,034,285 | 2.96 | 2.79 | 67 |
| 37 | 8,830,021 | 4.35 | 3.77 | 40 |
| 38 | 8,763,000 | 1.34 | 0.82 | 29 |
| 39 | 8,675,258 | 1.36 | 0.99 | 48 |
| 40 | 8,388,057 | 8.15 | 3.05 | 11 |
| 41 | 8,172,459 | * | * | 70 |
| 42 | 8,161,755 | n.a. | n.a. | 58 |
| 43 | 8,014,541 | * | 18.93 | 46 |
| 44 | 7,942,823 | 3.91 | 4.48 | 55 |
| 45 | 7,711,522 | * | 1.11 | 69 |
| 46 | 7,307,297 | 1.99 | 0.63 | 129 |
| 47 | 6,451,505 | n.a. | 1.29 | 52 |
| 48 | 6,218,075 | 2.04 | 2.04 | 9 |
| 49 | 6,207,296 | 1.79 | 1.68 | 38 |
| 50 | 5,957,240 | 5.40 | 4.31 | 60 |

*Company showed loss.

n.a. = Not available.

**Table 8B: Corporate Social Expenditures of 75 Largest Donors as a Percent of U.S. and Worldwide Pretax Income (continued)**

| Company Rank | Total Corporate Social Expenditure | Corporate Social Expenditure As A Percent of | | Rank for Corporate Assistance Only |
|---|---|---|---|---|
| | | U.S. Pretax Income | Worldwide Pretax Income | |
| 51 | 5,921,708 | * | * | 75 |
| 52 | 5,500,000 | 2.69 | 1.93 | 71 |
| 53 | 5,385,449 | 20.71 | 2.46 | 66 |
| 54 | 5,089,600 | * | 07.07 | 23 |
| 55 | 5,021,137 | 1.97 | 1.44 | 19 |
| 56 | 4,846,401 | 1.15 | 0.86 | 64 |
| 57 | 4,643,812 | 3.18 | 4.69 | 47 |
| 58 | 4,601,756 | 1.54 | 1.48 | 62 |
| 59 | 4,433,794 | * | * | 35 |
| 60 | 4,428,818 | 3.41 | 1.62 | 54 |
| 61 | 4,345,749 | 0.96 | 1.22 | 36 |
| 62 | 4,337,600 | 1.05 | 0.83 | 49 |
| 63 | 4,164,330 | n.a. | 0.77 | 59 |
| 64 | 3,920,411 | * | * | 124 |
| 65 | 3,914,331 | n.a. | n.a. | 45 |
| 66 | 3,823,691 | 3.37 | 3.37 | 31 |
| 67 | 3,781,629 | 0.18 | 0.18 | 65 |
| 68 | 3,560,000 | 1.01 | 1.01 | 63 |
| 69 | 3,363,048 | * | 23.82 | 103 |
| 70 | 3,299,798 | 2.97 | 2.14 | 53 |
| 71 | 3,270,357 | 1.38 | 1.13 | 169 |
| 72 | 3,176,393 | 0.20 | 0.20 | 145 |
| 73 | 3,108,419 | 1.54 | 1.13 | 37 |
| 74 | 3,014,211 | 1.03 | 1.03 | 127 |
| 75 | 2,848,559 | 1.27 | 1.00 | 105 |

*Company showed loss.

n.a. = Not available.

**Table 9A: Contributions as a Percent of U.S. Pretax Income, 1986—**
Companies Grouped by Dollar Size of Program

| Program Size | Number of Companies | Lower Quartile | Median | Upper Quartile |
|---|---|---|---|---|
| Under $500,000 | 67 | 0.02% | 0.78% | 1.42% |
| $500,000 to $1 million | 52 | 0.54 | 0.85 | 1.50 |
| $1 million to $5 million | 102 | 0.77 | 1.16 | 1.93 |
| $5 million and over | 66 | 1.24 | 2.16 | 4.16 |
| All Groups | 287 | 0.66 | 1.17 | 2.18 |

**Table 9B: Contributions as a Percent of Worldwide Pretax Income, 1986—**
Companies Grouped by Dollar Size of Program

| Program Size | Number of Companies | Lower Quartile | Median | Upper Quartile |
|---|---|---|---|---|
| Under $500,000 | 69 | 0.31% | 0.70% | 1.34% |
| $500,000 to $1 million | 58 | 0.51 | 0.84 | 1.35 |
| $1 million to $5 million | 114 | 0.69 | 1.01 | 1.45 |
| $5 million and over | 78 | 0.90 | 1.46 | 2.47 |
| All Groups | 319 | 0.59 | 1.01 | 1.63 |

**Table 10A: Contributions as a Percent of U.S. Pretax Income—Quartile Rank, 1986**
Companies Grouped by Size of U.S. Income

| | | Contributions Ratios[1] | | |
| U.S. Pretax Net Income | Number of Companies | Lower Quartile[2] | Median | Upper Quartile[2] |
|---|---|---|---|---|
| Below $5 million . . . . . . . . . . . . . . . . . . . . . . . . . . . . . . . . . | 1 | * | * | * |
| $5-9.9 million . . . . . . . . . . . . . . . . . . . . . . . . . . | 6 | 2.40 | 5.08 | 13.01 |
| $10-24.9 million . . . . . . . . . . . . . . . . . . . . . . . . . . . . . . . | 25 | 1.19 | 1.69 | 3.00 |
| $25-49.9 million . . . . . . . . . . . . . . . . . . . . . . . . . . . . . | 25 | 0.84 | 1.54 | 3.17 |
| $50-99.9 million . . . . . . . . . . . . . . . . . . . . . . . . . . . . . | 54 | 0.58 | 1.12 | 1.87 |
| $100-249.9 million . . . . . . . . . . . . . . . . . . . . . . . . . . . | 79 | 0.58 | 1.01 | 1.91 |
| $250-499.9 million . . . . . . . . . . . . . . . . . . . . . . . . . . | 46 | 0.54 | 1.03 | 2.39 |
| $500-999.9 million . . . . . . . . . . . . . . . . . . . . . . . . . . | 33 | 0.33 | 1.06 | 1.49 |
| $1 billion and over . . . . . . . . . . . . . . . . . . . . . . . . . . | 18 | 0.24 | 0.92 | 2.03 |
| **All Income Groups** . . . . . . . . . . . . . . . . . . . . . . . . . | **287** | **0.66** | **1.17** | **2.18** |

[1]The statistics presented here are derived only from companies with positive income.
[2]This is the 75th percentile.
*Categories with fewer than 5 cases have been excluded.

**Table 10B: Contributions as a Percent of Worldwide Pretax Income—Quartile Rank, 1986**
Companies Grouped by Size of Worldwide Income

| | | Contributions Ratios[1] | | |
| Worldwide Pretax Income | Number of Companies | Lower Quartile | Median | Upper Quartile[2] |
|---|---|---|---|---|
| Below $5 million . . . . . . . . . . . . . . . . . . . . . . . . . . . . . . . . . | 1 | * | * | * |
| $5-9.9 million . . . . . . . . . . . . . . . . . . . . . . . . . . . . . . . . . . . | 5 | 2.34 | 3.93 | 18.52 |
| $10-24.9 million . . . . . . . . . . . . . . . . . . . . . . . . . . . . . . . . . | 29 | 1.04 | 1.61 | 3.68 |
| $25-49.9 million . . . . . . . . . . . . . . . . . . . . . . . . . . . . . . . . . | 24 | 0.81 | 1.37 | 2.20 |
| $50-99.9 million . . . . . . . . . . . . . . . . . . . . . . . . . . . . . . . . . | 48 | 0.64 | 1.12 | 1.71 |
| $100-249.9 million . . . . . . . . . . . . . . . . . . . . . . . . . . . . . . . | 83 | 0.52 | 0.89 | 1.43 |
| $250-499.9 million . . . . . . . . . . . . . . . . . . . . . . . . . . . . . . . | 55 | 0.49 | 0.95 | 1.42 |
| $500-999.9 million . . . . . . . . . . . . . . . . . . . . . . . . . . . . . . . | 38 | 0.33 | 0.85 | 1.27 |
| $1 billion and over . . . . . . . . . . . . . . . . . . . . . . . . . . . . | 36 | 0.46 | 0.82 | 1.39 |
| **All Income Groups** . . . . . . . . . . . . . . . . . . . . . . . . . | **319** | **0.59** | **1.01** | **1.63** |

[1]The statistics presented here are derived only from companies with positive income.
[2]This is the 75th percentile.
*Categories with fewer than 5 cases have been excluded.

## Table 11A: Contributions as a Percent of U.S. Pretax Income—Quartile Rank, 1986
Companies Grouped by Industry Class (with at least five cases in each)

| Industrial Classification | Number of Companies | Contributions Ratios[1] | | |
|---|---|---|---|---|
| | | Lower Quartile | Median | Upper Quartile[2] |
| Chemicals | 24 | 0.84% | 1.01% | 2.75% |
| Electrical machinery and equipment | 24 | 0.94 | 2.02 | 4.63 |
| Fabricated metal products | 5 | 0.49 | 1.06 | 2.13 |
| Food, beverage and tobacco | 20 | 0.83 | 1.78 | 3.11 |
| Machinery, nonelectrical | 9 | 1.16 | 1.29 | 2.93 |
| Paper and like products | 11 | 0.65 | 0.91 | 1.34 |
| Petroleum and gas[3] | 14 | 1.33 | 2.37 | 3.92 |
| Pharmaceuticals | 8 | 1.08 | 1.30 | 4.15 |
| Primary metal industries | 5 | 0.39 | 1.41 | 10.30 |
| Printing and publishing | 5 | 0.85 | 1.42 | 2.61 |
| Stone, clay and glass products | 6 | 0.26 | 0.76 | 5.08 |
| Textiles | 5 | 0.51 | 0.81 | 2.77 |
| Transportation equipment[4] | 10 | 1.18 | 1.69 | 3.69 |
| Banking | 40 | 0.88 | 1.33 | 1.62 |
| Business services[5] | 5 | 0.67 | 1.35 | 1.58 |
| Insurance | 30 | 0.75 | 1.03 | 1.97 |
| Retail and wholesale trade | 11 | 0.66 | 1.03 | 2.61 |
| Telecommunications | 9 | 0.29 | 0.69 | 2.00 |
| Utilities | 41 | 0.20 | 0.31 | 0.48 |

[1]The statistics presented here are derived only from companies with positive net income.
[2]This is the 75th percentile.
[3]Includes mining companies.
[4]Includes tire manufacturers.
[5]Includes engineering and construction companies.

## Table 11B: Contributions as a Percent of Worldwide Pretax Income—Quartile Rank, 1986
Companies Grouped by Industry Class (with at least five cases in each)

| Industrial Classification | Number of Companies | Contributions Ratios[1] | | |
|---|---|---|---|---|
| | | Lower Quartile | Median | Upper Quartile[2] |
| Chemicals | 26 | 0.61% | 1.14% | 1.60% |
| Electrical machinery and equipment | 26 | 0.90 | 1.32 | 2.60 |
| Fabricated metal products | 5 | 0.47 | 0.89 | 1.18 |
| Food, beverage and tobacco | 22 | 0.67 | 1.50 | 2.47 |
| Machinery, nonelectrical | 13 | 0.96 | 2.43 | 3.50 |
| Paper and like products | 11 | 0.66 | 0.74 | 1.20 |
| Petroleum and gas[3] | 18 | 0.83 | 1.18 | 1.61 |
| Pharmaceuticals | 9 | 0.75 | 0.89 | 1.44 |
| Primary metal industries | 5 | 0.35 | 1.41 | 9.18 |
| Printing and publishing | 9 | 0.94 | 1.42 | 2.04 |
| Stone, clay and glass products | 6 | 0.23 | 0.68 | 3.40 |
| Textiles and apparel | 5 | 0.49 | 0.75 | 2.57 |
| Transportation equipment[4] | 11 | 0.99 | 1.61 | 2.14 |
| Banking | 42 | 0.86 | 1.14 | 1.53 |
| Business services[5] | 6 | 0.63 | 0.92 | 1.35 |
| Insurance | 33 | 0.73 | 0.99 | 1.97 |
| Retail and wholesale trade | 12 | 0.59 | 1.02 | 1.24 |
| Telecommunications | 12 | 0.38 | 0.64 | 1.73 |
| Utilities | 42 | 0.20 | 0.27 | 0.51 |

[1]The statistics presented here are derived only from companies with positive net income.
[2]This is the 75th percentile.
[3]Includes mining companies.
[4]Includes tire manufacturers.
[5]Includes engineering and construction companies.

**Table 12A: Contributions as a Percent of U.S. Pretax Income—Quartile Rank, 1986**
Companies Grouped by Size of U.S. Assets

| Assets | Number of Companies | Contributions' Ratios[1] | | |
| --- | --- | --- | --- | --- |
| | | Lower Quartile | Median | Upper Quartile[2] |
| Below $100 million .............................. | 0 | * | * | * |
| $100-199 million .............................. | 7 | 1.21% | 1.41% | 3.22% |
| $200-299 million .............................. | 10 | 0.61 | 1.26 | 1.87 |
| $300-499 million .............................. | 13 | 0.56 | 1.03 | 2.00 |
| $500-999 million .............................. | 36 | 0.00 | 1.11 | 2.07 |
| $1-1.9 billion ........................................ | 50 | 0.54 | 1.05 | 2.43 |
| $2-2.9 billion ........................................ | 21 | 0.57 | 1.05 | 2.37 |
| $3-3.9 billion ........................................ | 22 | 0.65 | 0.93 | 2.08 |
| $4-4.9 billion ........................................ | 11 | 0.95 | 1.54 | 3.17 |
| $5-9.9 billion ........................................ | 46 | 0.72 | 1.28 | 1.93 |
| $10 billion and over ............................. | 49 | 0.63 | 1.26 | 2.41 |
| **All Asset Groups**.............................. | **265** | **0.67** | **1.17** | **2.16** |

[1]The statistics presented here are derived only from companies with positive net income.
[2]This is the 75th percentile.
*Categories with fewer than 5 cases are excluded.

**Table 12B: Contributions as a Percent of Worldwide Pretax Income—Quartile Rank, 1986**
Companies Grouped by Size of Worldwide Assets

| Assets | Number of Companies | Contributions' Ratios[1] | | |
| --- | --- | --- | --- | --- |
| | | Lower Quartile | Median | Upper Quartile[2] |
| Below $100 million .............................. | 1 | * | * | * |
| $100-199 million .............................. | 6 | 1.09% | 1.72% | 3.35% |
| $200-299 million .............................. | 8 | 0.67 | 1.15 | 1.50 |
| $300-499 million .............................. | 17 | 0.48 | 0.94 | 1.31 |
| $500-999 million .............................. | 33 | 0.63 | 1.37 | 2.14 |
| $1-1.9 billion ........................................ | 57 | 0.39 | 0.95 | 1.50 |
| $2-2.9 billion ........................................ | 28 | 0.58 | 0.78 | 2.20 |
| $3-3.9 billion ........................................ | 29 | 0.60 | 0.91 | 1.84 |
| $4-4.9 billion ........................................ | 15 | 0.79 | 0.95 | 1.51 |
| $5-9.9 billion ........................................ | 54 | 0.64 | 1.18 | 1.53 |
| $10 billion and over ............................. | 71 | 0.60 | 1.04 | 1.63 |
| **All Asset Groups**.............................. | **319** | **0.59** | **1.01** | **1.63** |

[1]The statistics presented here are derived only from companies with positive net income.
[2]This is the 75th percentile.
*Categories with fewer than 5 cases are excluded.

**Table 13A: Contributions as a Percent of U.S. Pretax Income, 1986**
Companies Grouped by Size of U.S. Sales

| U.S. Sales | Number of Companies | Lower Quartile | Median | Upper Quartile |
|---|---|---|---|---|
| Below $250 million ........................... | 5 | 1.19 | 1.42 | 3.60 |
| $250-$500 million ........................... | 13 | 0.58 | 1.06 | 3.20 |
| $500 million-$1 billion ........................... | 32 | 0.74 | 1.28 | 2.16 |
| $1 billion-$2.5 billion ........................... | 35 | 0.66 | 1.22 | 2.71 |
| $2.5 billion-$5 billion ........................... | 36 | 0.96 | 1.56 | 3.10 |
| $5 billion and over ........................... | 36 | 1.24 | 2.04 | 4.25 |
| Total ........................... | 157 | 0.86 | 1.43 | 3.01 |

**Table 13B: Contributions as a Percent of Worldwide Pretax Income, 1986**
Companies Grouped by Size of Worldwide Sales

| Worldwide Sales | Number of Companies | Lower Quartile[2] | Median | Upper Quartile |
|---|---|---|---|---|
| Below $250 million ........................... | 5 | 0.82 | 1.42 | 3.17 |
| $250-$500 million ........................... | 13 | 0.84 | 1.21 | 2.97 |
| $500 million-$1 billion ........................... | 35 | 0.62 | 1.12 | 1.77 |
| $1 billion-$2.5 billion ........................... | 50 | 0.58 | 0.98 | 2.14 |
| $2.5 billion-$5 billion ........................... | 41 | 0.75 | 0.99 | 1.51 |
| $5 billion and over ........................... | 56 | 0.91 | 1.32 | 2.00 |
| Total ........................... | 200 | 0.71 | 1.16 | 1.87 |

**Table 14: Comparison of Corporate Contributions, 1986 and 1985**
316 Companies Reporting in Both Years

| Beneficiary | 1986 | | 1985 | | Median Percent Change 1985-1986 |
|---|---|---|---|---|---|
| | Median Contributions Expenditure | Contributions to Beneficiary as Percent of Total Contributions (Median) | Median Contributions Expenditure | Contributions to Beneficiary as Percent of Total Contributions (Median) | |
| Health and human services ......... | $ 521,020 | 36.7% | $ 455,501 | 37.5% | 9.4% |
| Education ...................... | 442,585 | 31.0 | 398,549 | 29.3 | 12.2 |
| Culture and art .................. | 145,393 | 10.5 | 132,855 | 10.1 | 9.0 |
| Civic and community activities ....... | 155,425 | 11.7 | 146,498 | 11.3 | 6.7 |
| Other ......................... | 36,712 | 2.2 | 57,945 | 3.6 | −46.7 |
| Total ...................... | $1,398,922 | a | $1,373,981 | a | 8.7% |

[a]Since subcategory percentages are medians rather than sums, they do not add to 100 percent.

**Table 15: Beneficiaries of Company Support, 1986—**
Quartiles for Companies Grouped by Dollar Size of Program

| Program Size | Number of Companies | Health and Human Services | | | Education | | | Culture and Art | | |
|---|---|---|---|---|---|---|---|---|---|---|
| | | Lower Quartile | Median | Upper Quartile | Lower Quartile | Median | Upper Quartile | Lower Quartile | Median | Upper Quartile |
| Less than $500,000 ......... | 87 | 39.4% | 49.0% | 59.3% | 13.4% | 23.7% | 33.4% | 4.0% | 8.9% | 14.9% |
| $500,000 to $1 million ....... | 72 | 32.7 | 40.6 | 51.8 | 23.2 | 29.7 | 37.6 | 6.1 | 9.1 | 16.2 |
| $1 million to $5 million ...... | 126 | 26.1 | 35.3 | 45.4 | 23.0 | 33.1 | 40.7 | 7.3 | 11.4 | 18.5 |
| $5 million and over ......... | 85 | 18.5 | 26.1 | 34.9 | 26.4 | 38.8 | 49.0 | 5.4 | 11.6 | 17.4 |
| All Companies ............. | 370 | 26.9 | 38.2 | 48.4 | 21.0 | 31.0 | 41.8 | 5.7 | 10.5 | 17.3 |

| Program Size | Number of Companies | Civic and Community | | | Other | | |
|---|---|---|---|---|---|---|---|
| | | Lower Quartile | Median | Upper Quartile | Lower Quartile | Median | Upper Quartile |
| Less than $500,000 ......... | 87 | 5.4% | 9.8% | 16.0% | 0.4% | 2.3% | 5.4% |
| $500,000 to $1 million ....... | 72 | 5.5 | 11.7 | 16.5 | 0.3 | 1.3 | 3.9 |
| $1 million to $5 million ...... | 126 | 7.4 | 12.8 | 17.7 | 0.8 | 2.1 | 5.4 |
| $5 million and over ......... | 85 | 6.9 | 12.2 | 18.2 | 0.7 | 2.8 | 5.7 |
| All Companies ............. | 370 | 6.7 | 11.9 | 17.6 | 0.6 | 2.1 | 5.4 |

## Table 16: Beneficiaries of Corporate Support, 1977 to 1986

| | 1986 370 Companies | | 1985[1] 436 Companies | | 1984 415 Companies | | 1983[1] 471 Companies | |
|---|---|---|---|---|---|---|---|---|
| | Thousands of Dollars | % of Total | Thousands of Dollars | % of Total | Thousands of Dollars | % of Total | Thousands of Dollars | % of Total |
| **Health and Human Services** | | | | | | | | |
| Federated drives: | | | | | | | | |
| United Ways[c] | $ 223,678 | 13.4% | | | $ 191,353 | 13.2 | | |
| Other federated campaigns[c] | 2,266 | 0.1 | | | 2,538 | 0.2 | | |
| National health organizations | 69,774 | 4.3 | | | 16,427 | 1.1 | | |
| National human service organizations | 43,287 | 2.6 | | | 14,576 | 1.0 | | |
| National youth organizations[d] | 3,533 | 0.2 | | | 4,666 | 0.3 | | |
| Hospitals: | | | | | | | | |
| Capital grants | 17,339 | 1.0 | | | 24,666 | 1.7 | | |
| Operating grants | 10,281 | 0.6 | | | 7,092 | 0.5 | | |
| Employee matching gifts for hospitals | 2,609 | 0.2 | | | 1,920 | 0.1 | | |
| Local youth organizations[d] | $ 26,114 | 1.6 | | | 21,751 | 1.5 | | |
| Agencies for senior citizens and elderly[b] | | | | | | | | |
| Other local health and human service agencies | | | | | 71,206 | 4.9 | | |
| Capital grants excluding hospitals[a] | | | | | | | | |
| Employee matching gifts for health and human services[e] | 2,918 | 0.2 | | | 1,645 | 0.1 | | |
| Other local health agencies[g] | 22,683 | 1.4 | | | | | | |
| Other local human service agencies[g] | 50,929 | 3.0 | | | | | | |
| Subcategories unspecified | 42,239 | 2.5 | | | 42,107 | 2.9 | | |
| Total health and human services | $ 468,649 | 28.0% | 494,109 | 29.2% | 399,948 | 27.7 | 367,300 | 28.7 |
| **Education:** | | | | | | | | |
| Higher education institutions: | | | | | | | | |
| Unrestricted institutional operating grants | 70,019 | 4.8 | | | 38,719 | 2.7 | | |
| Student financial aid (funded through college or university) | 25,551 | 1.5 | | | 26,080 | 1.8 | | |
| Departmental grants[c] | 110,449 | 6.6 | | | 63,110 | 4.4 | | |
| Special project or research grants[c] | 88,157 | 5.3 | | | 112,143 | 7.8 | | |
| Capital grants | 87,210 | 6.0 | | | 30,309 | 2.1 | | |
| Employee matching gifts for higher education | 98,696 | 5.9 | | | 72,238 | 5.0 | | |
| Grants to state and national fund-raising groups | 19,019 | 1.1 | | | 13,014 | .9 | | |
| Precollege educational institutions: | | | | | | | | |
| Employee matching gifts for precollege education[f] | 8,740 | 0.5 | | | 3,756 | 0.3 | | |
| Public school support[c] | 16,932 | 1.0 | | | 13,737 | 1.0 | | |
| All other support[c] | 13,941 | 0.8 | | | 8,629 | 0.6 | | |
| Scholarships and fellowships (other than those reported above) | 37,145 | 2.2 | | | 22,991 | 1.6 | | |
| Education-related organizations: | | | | | | | | |
| Economic education | 12,875 | 0.8 | | | 11,684 | 0.8 | | |
| All other support | 17,813 | 1.1 | | | 17,090 | 1.2 | | |
| Other | 44,932 | 2.7 | | | 70,221 | 4.9 | | |
| Subcategories unspecified | 66,504 | 4.0 | | | 57,949 | 4.0 | | |
| Total education | 717,981 | 42.9 | 650,005 | 38.3 | 561,670 | 38.9 | 498,800 | 39.0 |
| **Culture and Art** | | | | | | | | |
| Music | 23,846 | 1.4 | | | 19,673 | 1.4 | | |
| Museums | 37,937 | 2.3 | | | 30,350 | 2.1 | | |
| Public TV and Radio | 21,631 | 1.3 | | | 18,677 | 1.3 | | |
| Arts Funds or Councils | 12,110 | 0.7 | | | 8,429 | 0.6 | | |
| Theaters | 13,975 | 0.8 | | | 9,358 | 0.6 | | |
| Cultural Centers | 11,187 | 0.7 | | | 14,637 | 1.0 | | |
| Dance | 4,696 | 0.3 | | | 3,495 | 0.2 | | |
| Libraries | 3,505 | 0.2 | | | 2,538 | 0.2 | | |
| Employee matching gifts for culture and art | 14,782 | 0.9 | | | 8,928 | 0.6 | | |
| Other | 16,066 | 1.0 | | | 16,076 | 1.1 | | |
| Subcategories unspecified | 39,019 | 2.3 | | | 22,549 | 1.6 | | |
| Total culture and art | 198,754 | 11.9 | 187,536 | 11.1 | 154,711 | 10.7 | 145,200 | 11.4 |
| **Civic and Community Activities** | | | | | | | | |
| Public policy organizations | 15,711 | 0.9 | | | 15,334 | 1.1 | | |
| National community improvement organizations[d] | 12,642 | 0.8 | | | 30,483 | 2.1 | | |
| National environment and ecology organizations[d] | 8,533 | 0.5 | | | 77,964 | 5.4 | | |
| National justice and law organizations:[d] | 3,131 | 0.2 | | | | | | |
| System research, reform, alternatives | | | | | 2,666 | 0.2 | | |
| Litigation, defense, advocacy | 1,872 | 0.1 | | | 1,653 | 0.1 | | |
| Other national organizations[d] | 10,555 | 0.6 | | | 7,602 | 0.5 | | |
| Municipal or statewide improvement[e] | 18,315 | 1.1 | | | 7,781 | 0.5 | | |
| Community improvement: | | | | | | | | |
| Neighborhood or community-based groups[c] | 17,214 | 1.0 | | | 13,860 | 1.0 | | |
| Housing | 8,327 | 0.5 | | | 14,378 | 1.0 | | |
| Economic development/employment[c] | 24,451 | 1.5 | | | 9,910 | 0.7 | | |
| Legal systems/services[d] | 2,030 | 0.1 | | | 1,790 | 0.1 | | |
| Local environment and ecology[d] | 27,420 | 1.6 | | | 19,149 | 1.3 | | |
| Other local organizations[d] | 24,600 | 1.5 | | | 36,426 | 2.5 | | |
| Subcategories unspecified | 45,678 | 2.7 | | | 32,606 | 2.3 | | |
| Total civic and community activities | 220,479 | 13.2 | 279,508 | 16.5 | 271,602 | 18.8 | 188,800 | 14.8 |
| **Other** | | | | | | | | |
| Religious activities | 604 | * | | | 513 | * | | |
| Women's causes[b] | | | | | 3,434 | 0.3 | | |
| Groups in U.S. whose principal objective is aid in other countries | 31,611 | 1.9 | | | 19,513 | 1.4 | | |
| Activities other than above | 19,252 | 1.2 | | | 27,819 | 1.9 | | |
| Subcategories unspecified | 16,652 | 1.0 | | | 8,538 | 0.6 | | |
| Total other | 68,118 | 4.0 | 83,549 | 4.9 | 56,383 | 3.9 | 78,000 | 6.1 |
| Grand Total | $1,673,982 | 100.0% | $1,694,707 | 100.0% | $1,444,313 | 100.0% | $1,278,400 | 100.0% |

[1]No data were collected on subcategories for 1979, 1981, 1983 and 1985. [2]Subcategory percentages do not add up to this total because of rounding. [3]Does not total 100 percent because of rounding. *Less than 0.1 percent. [a]Subcategory discontinued after 1982. [b]Subcategory used between 1978 and 1982. [c]Subcategory previously combined with another; treated separately in 1984. [d]Subcategory split into national and local components in 1984. [e]Subcategory introduced in 1984. [f]Subcategory introduced in 1978. [g]Subcategory previously combined with another; treated separately in 1986.

# Table 16: Beneficiaries of Corporate Support, 1976 to 1985 (continued)

| 1982 534 Companies | | 1981[1] 788 Companies | | 1980 732 Companies | | 1979[1] 786 Companies | | 1978 759 Companies | | 1977 814 Companies | |
|---|---|---|---|---|---|---|---|---|---|---|---|
| Thousands of Dollars | % of Total | Thousands of Dollars | % of Total | Thousands of Dollars | % of Total | Thousands of Dollars | % of Total | Thousands of Dollars | % of Total | Thousands of Dollars | % of Total |
| $ 182,384 | 14.2% | | | $170,652 | 17.1% | | | $142,085 | 20.5% | $128,511 | 21.6% |
| 9,831 | 0.8 | | | 11,362 | 1.1 | | | 6,551 | 0.9 | 4,763 | 0.8 |
| 15,226 | 1.2 | | | 5,434 | 0.5 | | | 4,495 | 0.7 | 5,409 | 0.9 |
| 26,985 | 2.1 | | | 29,848 | 3.0 | | | 24,548 | 3.5 | 23,632 | 4.0 |
| 10,694 | 0.8 | | | 11,063 | 1.1 | | | 6,138 | 0.9 | 5,433 | 0.9 |
| 2,157 | 0.2 | | | 749 | 0.1 | | | 292 | * | 202 | |
| 30,517 | 2.4 | | | 29,710 | 3.0 | | | 21,892 | 3.2 | 19,216 | 3.2 |
| 3,964 | 0.3 | | | 3,467 | 0.3 | | | 1,690 | 0.2 | — | — |
| 44,603 | 3.5 | | | 41,724 | 4.2 | | | 28,328 | 4.1 | 25,027 | 4.2 |
| 70,946 | 5.5 | | | — | — | | | — | — | — | — |
| | | | | 33,857 | 3.4 | | | 19,832 | 2.9 | 15,367 | 2.6 |
| $ 397,305 | 31.0 | $ 393,309 | 33.6% | 337,866 | 34.0[2] | 292,641 | 35.0 | 225,851 | 36.9 | 227,620 | 38.3[2] |
| 57,352 | 4.5 | | | 55,964 | 5.6 | | | 43,826 | 6.3 | 34,780 | 5.9 |
| 23,154 | 1.8 | | | 15,266 | 1.5 | | | 13,347 | 1.9 | 12,663 | 2.1 |
| 114,562 | 8.9 | | | 64,685 | 6.5 | | | 41,816 | 6.0 | 31,559 | 5.3 |
| 46,845 | 3.7 | | | 46,374 | 4.7 | | | 32,428 | 4.7 | 31,067 | 5.2 |
| 71,167 | 5.5 | | | 45,418 | 4.6 | | | 25,229 | 3.6 | 22,449 | 3.8 |
| 17,381 | 1.3 | | | 14,854 | 1.5 | | | 12,068 | 1.7 | 10,929 | 1.8 |
| 5,197 | 0.4 | | | 3,403 | 0.3 | | | 1,852 | 0.3 | — | — |
| 14,028 | 1.1 | | | 9,287 | 0.9 | | | 5,209 | 0.7 | 6,434 | 1.1 |
| 34,568 | 2.7 | | | 31,180 | 3.1 | | | 20,353 | 2.9 | 18,711 | 3.1 |
| 23,896 | 1.9 | | | 15,135 | 1.5 | | | 11,488 | 1.7 | 7,694 | 1.3 |
| 28,158 | 2.2 | | | 18,170 | 1.8 | | | 11,587 | 1.7 | 13,715 | 2.3 |
| 40,908 | 3.2 | | | 21,464 | 2.2 | | | 17,649 | 2.5 | 15,226 | 2.6 |
| 44,997 | 3.5 | | | 34,647 | 3.5 | | | 19,408 | 2.8 | 14,776 | 2.5 |
| 522,213 | 40.7 | 429,810 | 36.7 | 375,847 | 37.8[2] | 314,845 | 37.7 | 256,260 | 37.0[2] | 220,003 | 37.0 |
| 19,492 | 1.5 | | | 14,664 | 1.5 | | | 10,071 | 1.5 | 7,432 | 1.3 |
| 31,714 | 2.5 | | | 23,336 | 2.4 | | | 17,164 | 2.5 | 11,819 | 2.0 |
| 18,346 | 1.4 | | | 16,310 | 1.6 | | | 11,299 | 1.6 | 9,493 | 1.6 |
| 9,341 | 0.7 | | | 9,032 | 0.9 | | | 5,608 | 0.8 | 4,536 | 0.8 |
| 10,062 | 0.8 | | | 7,042 | 0.7 | | | 4,008 | 0.6 | 3,445 | 0.6 |
| 10,533 | 0.8 | | | 11,361 | 1.1 | | | 6,686 | 1.0 | 5,308 | 0.9 |
| 4,238 | 0.3 | | | 3,182 | 0.3 | | | 1,516 | 0.2 | 774 | 0.1 |
| 2,974 | 0.2 | | | 2,670 | 0.3 | | | 2,193 | 0.3 | 2,011 | 0.3 |
| 4,312 | 0.4 | | | 2,065 | 0.2 | | | 402 | * | 191 | * |
| 14,272 | 1.1 | | | 8,011 | 0.8 | | | 5,120 | 0.7 | 3,583 | 0.6 |
| 20,554 | 1.6 | | | 11,000 | 1.1 | | | 5,939 | 0.9 | 4,576 | 0.8 |
| 145,838 | 11.4[2] | 139,620 | 11.9 | 108,673 | 10.9 | 82,509 | 9.9 | 70,006 | 10.1 | 53,168 | 9.0 |
| 15,220 | 1.2 | | | 16,031 | 1.6 | | | 7,921 | 1.1 | 7,016 | 1.2 |
| 48,214 | 3.8 | | | 47,034 | 4.7 | | | 28,779 | 4.2 | 26,321 | 4.4 |
| 13,783 | 1.1 | | | 10,794 | 1.1 | | | 11,190 | 1.6 | 15,097 | 2.5 |
| 7,001 | 0.5 | | | 6,065 | 0.6 | | | 3,317 | 0.5 | 3,122 | 0.5 |
| 12,751 | 1.0 | | | 7,711 | 0.8 | | | 5,627 | 0.8 | 2,655 | 0.5 |
| 27,683 | 2.2 | | | 14,863 | 1.5 | | | 11,714 | 1.7 | 9,809 | 1.7 |
| 24,600 | 1.9 | | | 14,290 | 1.4 | | | 10,464 | 1.5 | 4,269 | 0.7 |
| 149,252 | 11.7 | 136,647 | 11.7 | 116,788 | 11.7 | 97,345 | 11.6 | 79,012 | 11.4 | 68,289 | 11.5 |
| 1,396 | 0.1 | | | 1,616 | 0.2 | | | 1,493 | 0.3 | 1,832 | 0.3 |
| 3,434 | 0.3 | | | 2,791 | 0.3 | | | 1,721 | 0.2 | — | — |
| 18,555 | 1.4 | | | 17,348 | 1.7 | | | 6,644 | 1.0 | 5,803 | 1.0 |
| 36,532 | 2.8 | | | 23,167 | 2.3 | | | 18,326 | 2.6 | 15,560 | 2.6 |
| 7,081 | 0.6 | | | 10,529 | 1.1 | | | 3,859 | 0.5 | 1,593 | 0.3 |
| 66,998 | 5.2 | 71,304 | 6.1 | 55,451 | 5.6 | 48,256 | 5.8 | 32,043 | 4.5 | 32,482 | 4.2 |
| $1,281,606 | 100.0 | $1,170,688 | 100.0% | 994,626 | 100.0% | $835,596 | 100.0% | $693,172 | 100.0% | $593,868 | 100.0% |

**Table 17: Beneficiaries of Company Support, 1986**—Quartiles for Companies Grouped by Industry Class[1]

| Industrial Classification | Number of Companies | Health and Human Services | | | Education | | |
|---|---|---|---|---|---|---|---|
| | | Lower Quartile | Median | Upper Quartile | Lower Quartile | Median | Upper Quartile |
| Chemicals | 28 | 25.1% | 32.4% | 43.1% | 31.0% | 39.2% | 45.8% |
| Electrical machinery and equipment | 28 | 31.7 | 00.8 | 44.3 | 01.0 | 43.0 | 59.3 |
| Fabricated metals | 6 | 33.3 | 43.8 | 54.7 | 16.2 | 26.5 | 32.0 |
| Food, beverage and tobacco | 24 | 25.5 | 34.4 | 47.8 | 18.2 | 30.0 | 36.7 |
| Machinery, nonelectrical | 15 | 34.7 | 38.7 | 46.0 | 30.3 | 35.4 | 42.5 |
| Paper | 11 | 29.8 | 34.4 | 42.9 | 29.1 | 35.2 | 45.6 |
| Petroleum and gas[2] | 24 | 19.0 | 25.6 | 32.8 | 40.3 | 50.3 | 54.2 |
| Pharmaceuticals | 10 | 18.1 | 27.3 | 42.3 | 23.6 | 38.1 | 49.6 |
| Primary metals | 11 | 36.6 | 51.1 | 58.9 | 22.4 | 33.9 | 46.7 |
| Printing and publishing | 9 | 9.4 | 32.4 | 48.3 | 18.6 | 30.4 | 42.8 |
| Stone, clay and glass | 7 | 37.4 | 50.0 | 57.5 | 15.0 | 20.0 | 34.5 |
| Textiles and apparel | 6 | 27.5 | 40.4 | 49.9 | 29.7 | 47.3 | 58.0 |
| Transportation equipment[3] | 11 | 19.6 | 27.0 | 40.7 | 30.2 | 36.6 | 43.3 |
| Total: Manufacturing | 190 | 24.1 | 33.8 | 44.7 | 28.2 | 36.7 | 47.8 |
| Banking | 47 | 32.7 | 44.9 | 53.7 | 12.9 | 21.9 | 27.6 |
| Business services[4] | 8 | 29.5 | 39.5 | 47.7 | 26.4 | 31.1 | 45.9 |
| Finance | 5 | 19.1 | 28.6 | 40.7 | 27.5 | 36.6 | 40.6 |
| Insurance | 42 | 27.0 | 37.8 | 51.6 | 19.6 | 31.6 | 36.2 |
| Retail and wholesale trade | 15 | 35.4 | 43.7 | 56.6 | 13.9 | 21.0 | 30.8 |
| Telecommunications | 13 | 14.7 | 31.1 | 39.6 | 20.7 | 26.3 | 43.5 |
| Transportation | 5 | 29.3 | 44.7 | 52.0 | 25.0 | 27.8 | 30.8 |
| Utilities | 45 | 36.5 | 45.7 | 60.0 | 14.7 | 23.3 | 32.6 |
| Total: Nonmanufacturing | 180 | 30.1 | 41.8 | 51.8 | 16.7 | 25.6 | 33.8 |
| Total: All Companies | 370 | 26.9 | 38.2 | 48.4 | 21.0 | 31.0 | 41.8 |

[1]For an explanation of quartiles, see Table 2.
[2]Includes mining companies.
[3]Includes tire manufacturers.
[4]Includes engineering and construction companies.

# Table 17: Beneficiaries of Company Support, 1986 (continued)

| Culture and Art | | | Civic and Community | | | Other | | |
|---|---|---|---|---|---|---|---|---|
| Lower Quartile | Median | Upper Quartile | Lower Quartile | Median | Upper Quartile | Lower Quartile | Median | Upper Quartile |
| 3.4% | 6.8% | 13.4% | 8.0% | 12.1% | 16.6% | 1.0% | 3.1% | 5.4% |
| 1.9 | 9.2 | 14.2 | 1.4 | 7.6 | 11.3 | 1.3 | 3.1 | 6.6 |
| 6.5 | 7.8 | 17.1 | 2.8 | 9.8 | 19.7 | 1.5 | 3.2 | 5.5 |
| 5.3 | 9.4 | 16.9 | 3.8 | 10.3 | 18.0 | 0.9 | 4.2 | 11.4 |
| 7.2 | 8.4 | 15.7 | 3.6 | 7.5 | 11.2 | 1.1 | 5.1 | 7.2 |
| 5.2 | 8.1 | 15.1 | 10.3 | 14.2 | 16.1 | 0.2 | 0.4 | 2.5 |
| 5.7 | 11.2 | 13.0 | 9.5 | 12.9 | 17.3 | 0.6 | 1.4 | 3.9 |
| 2.8 | 6.0 | 12.4 | 5.4 | 10.6 | 18.2 | 2.3 | 7.3 | 17.9 |
| 4.9 | 6.2 | 8.9 | 5.9 | 9.1 | 12.1 | 0.8 | 2.6 | 4.8 |
| 9.3 | 18.5 | 23.7 | 3.4 | 11.3 | 16.4 | 0.2 | 1.2 | 4.9 |
| 6.3 | 9.7 | 10.5 | 5.1 | 12.3 | 18.8 | 0.2 | 0.5 | 3.0 |
| 1.8 | 3.0 | 11.2 | 4.4 | 6.9 | 10.5 | 0.6 | 1.0 | 7.1 |
| 11.6 | 13.3 | 16.9 | 5.0 | 9.1 | 13.4 | 0.8 | 3.5 | 5.2 |
| 4.9 | 8.8 | 14.3 | 5.6 | 10.0 | 15.5 | 0.7 | 2.3 | 5.4 |
| 10.4 | 14.0 | 19.3 | 8.6 | 16.0 | 20.0 | 0.8 | 3.1 | 5.9 |
| 4.4 | 5.5 | 18.6 | 5.0 | 8.0 | 15.0 | 1.2 | 2.8 | 19.0 |
| 11.8 | 15.8 | 20.7 | 9.7 | 12.5 | 21.8 | 2.4 | 4.1 | 10.5 |
| 7.7 | 12.3 | 20.0 | 5.0 | 10.4 | 15.8 | 0.3 | 1.0 | 3.4 |
| 5.5 | 8.1 | 12.3 | 8.9 | 15.3 | 24.4 | 0.2 | 1.6 | 7.2 |
| 10.1 | 17.3 | 27.9 | 10.3 | 16.9 | 20.9 | 1.4 | 2.6 | 6.0 |
| 9.2 | 19.1 | 21.7 | 7.4 | 17.7 | 20.1 | * | * | * |
| 4.1 | 8.0 | 13.8 | 8.1 | 15.0 | 24.2 | 0.2 | 1.5 | 4.8 |
| 7.6 | 11.9 | 19.2 | 7.9 | 14.3 | 19.7 | 0.5 | 2.0 | 5.4 |
| 5.7 | 10.5 | 17.3 | 6.7 | 11.9 | 17.6 | 0.6 | 2.1 | 5.4 |

# Table 18: Beneficiaries of Company Support, 1986—Companies Grouped by Industry Class (with at least five cases in each)

Percentage Distribution

| Industrial Classification | Number of Companies | Total Giving ($ Thousands) | National Health | National Human Service | National Youth | Federated Campaigns United Ways | Federated Campaigns Other | Hospital Capital Grants | Hospital Operating Grants | Hospital Matching Gifts | Local Youth | Matching Gifts | Other Health Service | Other Human Service | Unspecified | Total Health and Human Services |
|---|---|---|---|---|---|---|---|---|---|---|---|---|---|---|---|---|
| Chemicals | 28 | $ 156,391 | 1.2 | 1.0 | 0.1 | 10.4 | * | 1.2 | 0.5 | 0.1 | 1.3 | 0.1 | 2.6 | 7.0 | 1.1 | 26.5 |
| Electrical machinery | 28 | 298,091 | 0.5 | 0.8 | 0.2 | 14.1 | * | 1.2 | 0.4 | 0.3 | 1.4 | 0.1 | 1.5 | 1.5 | 0.3 | 22.2 |
| Fabricated metals | 6 | 4,794 | 0.4 | 0.1 | 0.1 | 20.0 | — | 0.4 | 6.0 | — | 1.1 | — | 1.7 | 1.3 | 7.5 | 38.6 |
| Food, beverage and tobacco | 24 | 198,909 | 0.4 | 14.5 | 0.2 | 4.8 | 0.1 | 0.7 | 0.2 | 0.1 | 0.8 | 0.2 | 0.4 | 3.1 | 9.8 | 35.4 |
| Machinery, nonelectrical | 15 | 24,859 | 0.4 | 0.1 | 0.1 | 19.3 | 0.8 | 0.6 | 0.7 | 0.1 | 1.1 | 0.7 | 0.8 | 1.5 | 10.8 | 37.0 |
| Paper and like products | 11 | 18,818 | 0.2 | 0.4 | 0.1 | 20.0 | 0.1 | 1.8 | 0.4 | * | 5.5 | 0.1 | 4.1 | 3.4 | 0.2 | 36.4 |
| Petroleum and gas[a] | 24 | 231,611 | 0.6 | 0.4 | 0.2 | 9.7 | 0.1 | 0.8 | 0.5 | 0.2 | 1.6 | 0.5 | 1.7 | 2.4 | 1.7 | 20.3 |
| Pharmaceuticals | 10 | 76,213 | 10.5 | 2.8 | 0.5 | 9.5 | 0.7 | 0.4 | 2.9 | 0.4 | 0.8 | 0.1 | 0.5 | 0.8 | * | 29.8 |
| Primary metals | 11 | 16,393 | 1.5 | 0.6 | 0.4 | 20.4 | * | 2.2 | 0.9 | — | 3.8 | — | 2.7 | 3.5 | — | 36.2 |
| Printing and publishing | 9 | 28,537 | 0.5 | 0.2 | 0.1 | 10.6 | 0.2 | 0.2 | 0.3 | * | 1.2 | * | 0.5 | 2.5 | 0.6 | 17.0 |
| Stone, clay and glass | 7 | 10,174 | 0.2 | 0.6 | 0.5 | 8.1 | * | 0.6 | 0.3 | 0.3 | 1.3 | — | 1.1 | 1.3 | 13.4 | 27.7 |
| Textiles and apparel | 6 | 6,399 | 0.7 | 0.4 | 0.6 | 12.3 | 0.8 | 1.2 | 0.4 | — | 5.7 | — | 1.5 | 4.9 | — | 28.3 |
| Transportation equipment[b] | 11 | 134,105 | 1.2 | 0.8 | 0.3 | 13.9 | — | 1.4 | 0.4 | — | 2.4 | — | 0.6 | 1.4 | 1.3 | 23.7 |
| Total: Manufacturing | 190 | 1,205,295 | 1.3 | 3.1 | 0.2 | 11.1 | 0.1 | 1.0 | 0.6 | 0.2 | 1.5 | 0.2 | 1.4 | 2.7 | 2.7 | 25.9 |
| Banking | 47 | 105,511 | 0.6 | 0.5 | 0.1 | 20.7 | 0.1 | 1.7 | 1.1 | 0.2 | 2.1 | 0.1 | 1.5 | 5.3 | 3.2 | 37.4 |
| Business services[c] | 8 | 10,705 | 3.7 | 3.4 | 1.1 | 12.2 | 1.5 | 1.0 | 0.1 | — | 3.0 | * | 4.1 | 3.4 | — | 33.6 |
| Finance | 5 | 10,345 | 1.3 | 2.1 | * | 8.5 | * | 2.3 | 2.8 | 0.3 | 1.3 | — | 1.5 | 5.1 | — | 25.3 |
| Insurance | 42 | 103,444 | 1.7 | 1.4 | 0.3 | 15.8 | * | 1.1 | 0.8 | * | 1.4 | 0.3 | 2.3 | 3.3 | 1.0 | 29.3 |
| Retail and wholesale trade | 15 | 64,573 | 2.2 | 1.3 | 0.4 | 22.9 | 0.1 | 0.4 | 0.2 | * | 1.1 | 0.1 | 0.2 | 6.8 | 1.2 | 36.8 |
| Telecommunications | 13 | 116,079 | 0.6 | 0.6 | 0.2 | 18.5 | 0.3 | 1.0 | 0.3 | * | 1.2 | — | 0.8 | 1.5 | 2.5 | 27.6 |
| Transportation | 5 | 6,855 | 0.1 | 0.4 | 0.1 | 17.4 | * | 0.2 | * | 0.3 | 2.9 | 0.1 | 0.4 | 9.1 | 0.9 | 32.0 |
| Utilities | 45 | 51,176 | 0.2 | 3.9 | 0.1 | 23.8 | 0.6 | 1.7 | 1.2 | * | 2.9 | 0.2 | 1.3 | 3.7 | 3.5 | 43.3 |
| Total: Nonmanufacturing | 180 | 468,687 | 1.1 | 1.3 | 0.2 | 19.2 | 0.2 | 1.2 | 0.7 | 0.1 | 1.7 | 0.1 | 1.4 | 3.9 | 2.1 | 33.3 |
| Total: All Companies | 370 | $1,673,982 | 1.2 | 2.6 | 0.2 | 13.4 | 0.1 | 1.0 | 0.6 | 0.2 | 1.6 | 0.2 | 1.4 | 3.0 | 2.5 | 28.0 |

[a] Includes mining companies.
[b] Includes tire manufacturers.
[c] Includes engineering and construction companies.
* Less than 0.1 percent.
Details in a row may not add to total due to rounding.

# Table 18: Beneficiaries of Company Support, 1986—Companies Grouped by Industry Class (with at least five cases in each) (continued)

Percentage Distribution

| Industrial Classification | Unrestricted Operating Grants | Student Financial Aid | Departmental Grants | Special Project or Research Grants | Capital Grants | Matching Gifts | State & National Fund-Raising Groups | Precollege Educational Institutions Matching Gifts | Public School Support | All Other Support | Scholarships and Fellowships | Education Related Organizations Economic Education | All Other Support | Other | Unspecified | Total Education[1] |
|---|---|---|---|---|---|---|---|---|---|---|---|---|---|---|---|---|
| Chemicals | 3.4 | 1.5 | 10.5 | 2.3 | 5.3 | 4.7 | 0.9 | 0.4 | 0.3 | 1.1 | 4.0 | 1.3 | 0.7 | 5.1 | 0.5 | 42.0 |
| Electrical machinery | 2.1 | 1.5 | 15.1 | 18.7 | 0.9 | 6.6 | 0.7 | 0.1 | 1.0 | 2.3 | 3.0 | 0.4 | 1.0 | 6.3 | 0.6 | 60.1 |
| Fabricated metals | 6.8 | — | — | — | — | 6.3 | 0.3 | — | * | * | 0.3 | 3.4 | 0.2 | — | 5.2 | 22.5 |
| Food, beverage and tobacco | 0.9 | 0.3 | 0.7 | 0.3 | 20.9 | 3.7 | 0.4 | 0.3 | 0.3 | 0.2 | 1.2 | 0.3 | 0.1 | 0.6 | 10.4 | 40.6 |
| Machinery, nonelectrical | 2.4 | 7.9 | 1.6 | 0.8 | 1.3 | 7.0 | 0.7 | 1.7 | 0.1 | 0.3 | 1.4 | 0.8 | 0.4 | 2.7 | 11.8 | 40.8 |
| Paper and like products | 4.1 | 2.3 | 3.0 | 2.2 | 6.0 | 4.7 | 0.8 | 0.5 | 2.2 | 0.4 | 4.1 | 1.5 | 0.2 | 2.0 | 0.9 | 34.7 |
| Petroleum and gas | 3.6 | 2.7 | 5.9 | 5.4 | 2.6 | 10.8 | 0.5 | 1.2 | 3.2 | 0.3 | 2.1 | 1.0 | 2.5 | 0.9 | 6.1 | 48.8 |
| Pharmaceuticals | 2.2 | 0.7 | 3.1 | 5.4 | 5.9 | 4.6 | 9.6 | 0.7 | 1.5 | 0.6 | 3.5 | 0.4 | 1.6 | 1.0 | 0.2 | 41.2 |
| Primary metals | 2.6 | 4.1 | 3.1 | 5.5 | 6.5 | 10.0 | 1.0 | 0.1 | 0.6 | 0.4 | 3.2 | 1.0 | 2.1 | * | 1.1 | 41.4 |
| Printing and publishing | 1.4 | 0.7 | 1.7 | 1.8 | 0.5 | 7.9 | 0.5 | 2.7 | 0.3 | 0.3 | 2.1 | 0.3 | 1.2 | 26.1 | 4.8 | 52.3 |
| Stone, clay and glass | 0.6 | 0.7 | 1.3 | 0.8 | 0.3 | 5.9 | 0.2 | 1.6 | 0.8 | * | 2.8 | 0.7 | 1.0 | — | 8.4 | 24.9 |
| Textiles and apparel | 3.6 | 1.5 | 22.2 | 0.8 | 4.2 | 7.9 | 2.1 | 0.7 | 0.8 | 4.5 | 4.5 | 1.4 | 3.3 | — | — | 57.4 |
| Transportation equipment | 22.1 | 0.5 | 4.7 | 0.6 | 3.8 | 4.1 | 0.6 | 0.4 | 0.4 | 0.6 | 3.2 | 1.4 | 0.9 | 0.5 | 3.2 | 47.2 |
| Total: Manufacturing | 4.6 | 1.5 | 7.4 | 6.6 | 5.9 | 6.3 | 1.2 | 0.6 | 1.1 | 1.0 | 2.7 | 0.8 | 1.1 | 3.3 | 4.0 | 48.1 |
| Banking | 4.3 | 0.8 | 0.4 | 0.4 | 5.3 | 5.2 | 0.6 | 0.9 | 0.7 | 0.6 | 0.8 | 0.7 | 0.3 | 0.3 | 4.4 | 25.8 |
| Business services | 2.6 | 0.1 | 7.4 | 5.9 | 0.6 | 14.1 | 0.8 | 0.3 | 0.1 | 0.3 | 3.3 | 0.5 | 1.3 | 1.3 | 0.3 | 39.1 |
| Finance | 5.2 | * | 2.4 | 0.7 | 0.8 | 8.1 | 0.6 | * | 2.2 | 0.7 | 4.7 | 1.3 | 2.2 | 0.9 | 7.8 | 37.6 |
| Insurance | 1.7 | 2.5 | 3.4 | 1.6 | 2.0 | 6.9 | 1.0 | 0.8 | 1.4 | 0.4 | 1.4 | 0.6 | 1.2 | 2.0 | 0.6 | 27.5 |
| Retail and wholesale trade | 2.0 | 1.4 | 0.3 | 0.9 | 2.5 | 1.2 | 0.3 | 0.1 | 0.7 | 0.1 | 0.7 | 0.3 | 0.4 | 1.0 | 8.3 | 20.0 |
| Telecommunications | 2.6 | 2.4 | 13.8 | 3.7 | 4.4 | 3.9 | 1.6 | — | 0.2 | 0.8 | 0.3 | 1.0 | 1.7 | 0.6 | 4.0 | 40.9 |
| Transportation | 2.2 | 0.3 | 0.3 | 6.5 | 3.1 | 2.5 | 5.4 | 1.6 | 0.1 | 2.6 | 3.2 | 0.4 | 0.1 | 0.4 | 0.7 | 29.5 |
| Utilities | 5.4 | 0.3 | 1.2 | 0.6 | 2.4 | 3.7 | 0.6 | 0.2 | 0.3 | 0.3 | 1.1 | 1.0 | 0.1 | 2.2 | 5.2 | 24.8 |
| Total: Nonmanufacturing | 3.1 | 1.6 | 4.7 | 1.8 | 3.4 | 4.8 | 1.0 | 0.4 | 0.7 | 0.5 | 1.0 | 0.8 | 0.9 | 1.1 | 4.0 | 29.6 |
| Total: All Companies | 4.2 | 1.5 | 6.6 | 5.3 | 5.2 | 5.9 | 1.1 | 0.5 | 1.0 | 0.8 | 2.2 | 0.8 | 1.1 | 2.7 | 4.0 | 42.9 |

[1]See footnotes on page 54.

**Table 18: Beneficiaries of Company Support, 1986—Companies Grouped by Industry Class (with at least five cases in each) (continued)**

| Industry Classification | Music | Museums | Public TV and Radio | Arts Funds or Councils | Theater | Cultural Centers | Dance | Libraries | Matching Gifts | Other | Unspecified | Total Culture and Art |
|---|---|---|---|---|---|---|---|---|---|---|---|---|
| | | | | | | *Percentage Distribution* | | | | | | |
| Chemicals | 0.9% | 1.5% | 0.5% | 0.7% | 1.1% | 0.3% | 0.1% | 0.1% | 0.4% | 0.5% | 0.3% | 6.4 |
| Electrical machinery | 0.7 | 2.0 | 1.9 | 0.4 | 0.4 | 0.4 | 0.1 | 0.2 | 1.8 | 0.8 | 0.1 | 8.9 |
| Fabricated metals | 1.2 | 4.1 | 0.5 | 1.1 | 0.5 | 1.5 | 0.2 | 0.1 | 0.6 | 9.6 | 1.3 | 20.6 |
| Food, beverage and tobacco | 0.7 | 0.7 | 0.2 | 0.3 | 0.3 | 0.1 | 0.1 | * | 0.5 | 1.7 | 5.7 | 10.3 |
| Machinery, nonelectrical | 0.3 | 0.4 | 0.2 | 0.3 | 1.1 | 0.8 | 0.2 | — | 1.3 | 1.3 | 6.5 | 12.4 |
| Paper and like products | 0.8 | 4.4 | 1.9 | 1.8 | 0.9 | 0.8 | 0.1 | 0.2 | 0.3 | 0.5 | 0.1 | 11.7 |
| Petroleum and gas | 1.8 | 2.0 | 2.4 | 0.5 | 0.7 | 0.6 | 0.3 | 0.4 | 0.9 | 0.7 | 3.1 | 13.6 |
| Pharmaceuticals | 1.2 | 1.8 | 1.6 | 0.2 | 0.6 | 0.7 | 0.1 | 0.1 | 0.7 | 0.4 | — | 7.3 |
| Primary metals | 1.8 | 2.3 | 0.6 | 0.5 | 1.2 | 0.9 | 0.5 | 0.2 | 0.2 | 2.0 | 0.2 | 10.4 |
| Printing and publishing | 1.5 | 3.7 | 0.2 | 0.6 | 0.7 | 0.8 | 0.5 | 0.9 | 2.5 | 0.6 | 5.5 | 17.5 |
| Stone, clay and glass | 0.7 | 32.2 | 0.2 | 0.3 | 0.2 | 0.3 | 0.1 | 0.4 | 0.9 | 0.3 | 2.9 | 38.3 |
| Textiles and apparel | 0.2 | 0.8 | 0.1 | 0.7 | 0.4 | 0.5 | * | 0.2 | — | 0.3 | — | 3.2 |
| Transportation equipment | 1.3 | 4.4 | 0.2 | 0.6 | 1.0 | 0.5 | 0.2 | 0.3 | 0.5 | 0.5 | 0.7 | 10.0 |
| Total: Manufacturing | 1.1 | 2.3 | 1.2 | 0.5 | 0.6 | 0.4 | 0.2 | 0.2 | 0.9 | 0.9 | 2.0 | 10.3 |
| Banking | 2.7 | 3.2 | 0.7 | 1.1 | 1.3 | 1.6 | 0.7 | 0.2 | 1.0 | 0.6 | 3.6 | 16.7 |
| Business services | 2.7 | 1.8 | 0.4 | 1.2 | 1.5 | 3.0 | 0.3 | * | — | 2.0 | 1.0 | 13.9 |
| Finance | 0.6 | 2.2 | 0.4 | 0.9 | 0.9 | 1.4 | 0.4 | 0.3 | 0.1 | 1.2 | 5.4 | 13.6 |
| Insurance | 1.8 | 1.7 | 3.1 | 2.6 | 0.5 | 0.6 | 0.3 | 0.1 | 0.4 | 1.3 | 0.8 | 13.1 |
| Retail and wholesale trade | 4.2 | 2.1 | 2.1 | 0.8 | 2.7 | 0.9 | 0.7 | 0.1 | 0.2 | 2.3 | 3.7 | 20.0 |
| Telecommunications | 1.9 | 1.8 | 1.0 | 0.8 | 1.7 | 1.9 | 0.9 | 0.3 | 1.2 | 1.0 | 4.8 | 17.2 |
| Transportation | 3.2 | 11.8 | 0.2 | 0.9 | 1.1 | 1.6 | 0.4 | — | 1.2 | * | 0.4 | 20.8 |
| Utilities | 1.6 | 1.7 | 0.4 | 1.2 | 0.6 | 0.3 | 0.2 | 0.2 | 0.7 | 1.2 | 3.5 | 11.5 |
| Total: Nonmanufacturing | 2.3 | 2.3 | 1.5 | 1.3 | 1.3 | 1.2 | 0.6 | 0.2 | 0.7 | 1.2 | 3.2 | 15.9 |
| Total: All Companies | 1.4 | 2.3 | 1.3 | 0.7 | 0.8 | 0.7 | 0.3 | 0.2 | 0.9 | 1.0 | 2.3 | 11.9 |

¹See footnotes on page 54.

**Table 18: Beneficiaries of Company Support, 1986—Companies Grouped by Industry Class (with at least five cases in each) (continued)**

Columns 5–8 fall under the heading *Justice and Law*; columns 9–13 fall under the heading *Community Improvement*; columns 4–17 fall under the heading *Civic and Community Activities*. Values are a *Percentage Distribution*.

| Industrial Classification | National Public Policy Groups | National Community Improvement Groups | National Environment and Ecology | System Research and Reform | Litigation | Defense and Advocacy Groups | Other National Groups | Municipal or Statewide Improvement | Neighborhood or Community Based Groups | Housing | Economic Development/ Employment | Legal Systems Service | Local Environment and Ecology | Other Local Groups | Unspecified | Total Civic and Community[1] |
|---|---|---|---|---|---|---|---|---|---|---|---|---|---|---|---|---|
| Chemicals | 0.8 | 0.5 | 2.7 | 0.1 | 0.1 | 0.1 | 0.9 | 0.5 | 0.6 | 0.3 | 0.5 | 0.1 | 0.4 | 1.9 | 4.7 | 14.1 |
| Electrical machinery | 0.4 | 0.9 | 0.2 | 0.1 | 0.1 | 0.1 | 0.7 | 0.1 | 0.4 | 0.2 | 1.2 | 0.1 | 0.1 | 0.8 | 0.1 | 5.4 |
| Fabricated metals | 1.5 | 0.5 | — | 0.2 | 0.1 | 0.1 | — | 1.0 | 4.5 | 0.3 | 0.8 | 0.1 | 0.6 | 1.3 | 5.1 | 15.9 |
| Food, beverage and tobacco | 0.1 | 0.2 | 0.1 | * | * | * | 0.2 | 4.1 | 0.4 | * | 0.3 | * | 0.4 | 0.3 | 4.6 | 10.9 |
| Machinery, nonelectrical | 0.3 | 0.5 | 0.3 | * | * | * | 0.1 | 0.1 | 1.4 | 0.2 | 0.1 | * | * | 1.3 | 2.4 | 6.8 |
| Paper and like products | 0.7 | 0.5 | 2.2 | 0.3 | 0.2 | 0.1 | 1.3 | 0.8 | 3.7 | 0.2 | 0.7 | 0.2 | 1.1 | 3.1 | 0.7 | 15.6 |
| Petroleum and gas | 1.8 | 0.9 | 0.9 | 0.2 | 0.2 | 0.2 | 0.9 | 1.2 | 1.5 | 1.4 | 0.9 | 0.1 | 0.9 | 1.6 | 2.7 | 15.2 |
| Pharmaceuticals | 2.9 | 1.9 | 0.4 | 0.4 | 0.5 | 0.1 | 0.3 | 0.4 | 1.3 | 0.1 | 0.5 | * | 0.5 | 1.4 | 0.1 | 10.1 |
| Primary metals | 0.6 | 0.8 | 0.3 | 0.5 | 0.2 | 0.2 | 1.1 | 0.5 | 1.6 | 1.5 | 1.2 | 0.1 | 0.5 | 0.7 | 0.6 | 10.3 |
| Printing and publishing | 0.6 | 0.6 | 0.1 | 0.2 | 0.1 | 0.1 | 0.9 | 1.0 | 1.1 | 0.1 | 0.8 | * | 0.3 | 2.5 | 1.7 | 9.9 |
| Stone, clay and glass | 0.7 | 0.1 | 0.1 | 0.2 | 0.1 | 0.1 | 1.1 | 0.4 | 0.5 | — | * | * | 1.4 | 1.0 | 2.7 | 8.3 |
| Textiles and apparel | 0.5 | 0.2 | 0.2 | 0.1 | 0.1 | 0.1 | * | 0.1 | 0.8 | 0.2 | 0.3 | * | 0.3 | 6.8 | — | 9.7 |
| Transportation equipment | 1.5 | 0.6 | 0.1 | 0.3 | * | * | 0.5 | 0.8 | 1.1 | 0.1 | 6.9 | 0.2 | 1.7 | 1.1 | 0.4 | 15.2 |
| Total: Manufacturing | 1.0 | 0.7 | 0.7 | 0.2 | 0.1 | 0.1 | 0.6 | 1.2 | 0.9 | 0.4 | 1.4 | 0.1 | 0.6 | 1.2 | 2.1 | 11.2 |
| Banking | 1.3 | 0.4 | 0.1 | * | * |  | 0.3 | 1.4 | 1.6 | 1.5 | 2.1 | 0.1 | 1.4 | 1.6 | 3.7 | 15.7 |
| Business services | 1.5 | 1.1 | 0.5 | * | * | 0.1 | 0.5 | 0.7 | 1.3 | 0.4 | 0.2 | * | 0.1 | 1.0 | 2.9 | 10.3 |
| Finance | 1.8 | 0.6 | 0.2 | * | 0.2 | 0.2 | 3.3 | 0.9 | 0.3 | * | 0.2 | * | 0.3 | 1.8 | 9.3 | 19.0 |
| Insurance | 1.0 | 1.1 | 0.1 | 0.7 | 0.1 | 0.1 | 1.0 | 1.0 | 1.0 | 1.0 | 1.3 | 0.2 | 17.2 | 2.4 | 0.4 | 28.4 |
| Retail and wholesale trade | 0.2 | 0.9 | * | 0.1 | 0.1 | 0.1 | 0.3 | 0.4 | 2.0 | 0.5 | 2.8 | 0.3 | 0.2 | 1.3 | 11.9 | 20.9 |
| Telecommunications | 0.8 | 1.3 | 0.1 | 0.2 | 0.2 | 0.4 | 0.8 | 0.6 | 0.5 | 0.2 | 1.0 | * | 0.2 | 0.5 | 4.7 | 11.4 |
| Transportation | 0.6 | 0.1 | 0.2 | 0.2 | 0.2 | 0.5 | 0.8 | 0.6 | 1.0 | * | 4.7 | 0.1 | * | 8.0 | 0.8 | 17.7 |
| Utilities | 0.2 | 0.4 | 0.1 | 0.1 | 0.1 | 0.2 | 0.1 | 1.2 | 3.2 | 0.3 | 0.5 | 0.2 | 1.2 | 7.0 | 3.0 | 17.7 |
| Total: Nonmanufacturing | 0.9 | 0.9 | 0.1 | 0.2 | 0.2 | 0.2 | 0.6 | 0.9 | 1.4 | 0.7 | 1.5 | 0.1 | 4.3 | 2.1 | 4.3 | 18.4 |
| Total: All Companies | 0.9 | 0.8 | 0.5 | 0.2 | 0.1 | 0.1 | 0.6 | 1.1 | 1.0 | 0.5 | 1.5 | 0.1 | 1.6 | 1.5 | 2.7 | 13.2 |

[1]See footnotes on page 54.

**Table 18: Beneficiaries of Company Support, 1986—Companies Grouped by Industry Class (with at least five cases in each) (continued)**

| Industry Classification | Other Causes | | | | Total Other Causes[1] |
|---|---|---|---|---|---|
| | Religious Activities | Aid in Other Countries | Other | Unspecified | |
| | | *Percentage Distribution* | | | |
| Chemicals | * | 7.9% | 2.5% | 0.6% | 11.0% |
| Electrical machinery and equipment | * | 0.8 | 1.1 | 0.6 | 3.4 |
| Fabricated metals | 0.3% | 0.3 | 0.8 | 1.0 | 2.4 |
| Food, beverage and tobacco | * | 1.3 | 0.4 | 1.1 | 2.8 |
| Machinery, nonelectrical | * | 1.0 | 1.0 | 1.1 | 3.0 |
| Paper and like products | 0.1 | 0.1 | 0.4 | 1.0 | 1.6 |
| Petroleum and gas | * | 0.3 | 0.6 | 1.3 | 2.2 |
| Pharmaceuticals | 0.1 | 9.4 | 2.0 | 0.1 | 11.3 |
| Primary metals | * | 1.4 | * | 0.1 | 1.5 |
| Printing and publishing | * | 0.2 | 2.7 | 0.4 | 3.3 |
| Stone, clay, and glass | * | 0.1 | 0.1 | 0.6 | 0.8 |
| Textiles and apparel | 1.2 | * | 0.1 | — | 1.3 |
| Transportation equipment | — | 0.6 | 0.8 | 2.5 | 3.9 |
| Total: Manufacturing | * | 2.4 | 1.1 | 1.0 | 4.5 |
| Banking | 0.1 | 1.9 | 0.7 | 1.8 | 4.4 |
| Business services | 0.5 | 0.4 | 0.2 | 2.1 | 3.1 |
| Finance | 0.2 | * | 2.4 | 2.0 | 4.6 |
| Insurance | 0.1 | 0.1 | 1.5 | * | 1.7 |
| Retail and wholesale trade | * | * | 2.0 | 0.3 | 2.3 |
| Telecommunications | * | 0.2 | 1.7 | 1.0 | 2.9 |
| Transportation | * | — | — | — | * |
| Utilities | 0.1 | — | 0.9 | 1.9 | 2.8 |
| Total: Nonmanufacturing | 0.1 | 0.5 | 1.3 | 1.0 | 2.9 |
| Total: All Companies | * | 1.9 | 1.2 | 1.0 | 4.0 |

[1]See footnotes on page 54.